Johnson's®

Your Toddler

from 2 to 3 years

London, New York, Munich Melbourne, Delhi

Text by Harriet Griffey
For Josh and Robbie

Project editor Susannah Steel
Project art editors Claire Legemah, Glenda Fisher
Senior editor Julia North
US editors Jill Hamilton, Jane Perlmutter
Managing art editor Tracey Ward
Production controller Louise Daly
Photography Ruth Jenkinson
Art direction Sally Smallwood

First American Edition, 2002
2 4 6 8 10 9 7 5 3 1

Published in the United States by DK Publishing, Inc.,
95 Madison Avenue, New York, NY 10016

A Cataloging-in-Publication record is available from the
Library of Congress
ISBN 0-7894-8444-7

Reproduced by Colourscan Overseas Pt, Ltd, Singapore
Printed by Graphicom, Italy

See our complete catalog at
www.dk.com

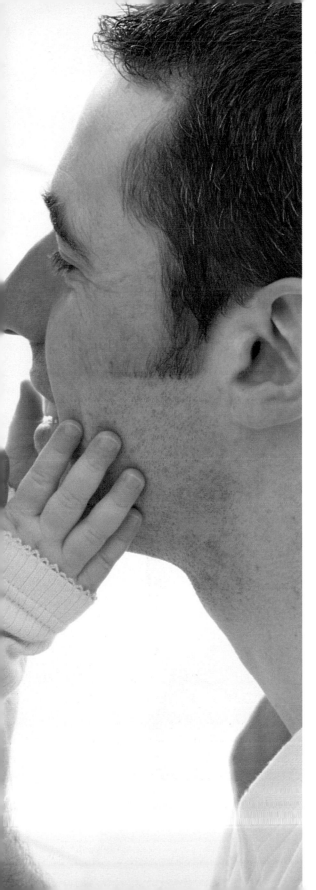

Contents

A message to parents from
Johnson&Johnson

For more than 100 years, Johnson & Johnson has been caring for babies. Our baby products help mothers and fathers soothe, comfort, and nurture a deep, loving bond with their child through everyday care.

Building on our commitment to children and families, Johnson & Johnson established the Johnson & Johnson Pediatric Institute, LLC. This unique organization promotes continued learning and research in pediatrics, infant development, and pregnancy, building programs and initiatives for professionals, parents, and caregivers that shape the future of children's health worldwide.

Through science, we continue to learn more about our youngest and their physical, cognitive, and emotional development. Parents and caregivers want advice on how to use this learning in their daily lives to complement their basic instincts to love, hold, and talk to their babies.

Good parenting is not a one-size-fits-all formula. With JOHNSON'S® *Child Development* series, we hope to support today's families with the knowledge, guidance, and understanding to help them bring forth the miracle embodied in each and every child.

The third year

The third year of
your child's life is
a wonderful time,
however challenging
it sometimes appears.
You will start to get a
real feel for your child's
developing character
as his language skills
increase and he
becomes interested
in more social
environments.

Your child's development

During this third year of her young life, your toddler will develop into a physically dexterous, verbally competent, and emotionally expressive individual personality. She will also begin to experience just what a magical, and sometimes frustrating, place the wider world can be.

Emerging independence

This is a time when your child progresses from being almost completely self-centered and limited in her outlook to becoming more aware of other people and events around her. It is also a time spent juggling your child's growing desire for greater independence and opportunity with the limits of her actual abilities, which can often be out of line with each other, and she will frequently require your help.

Growing closer

This can also be the best of times for you as a growing family. Sharing time together provides all sorts of learning opportunities as well as being fun – whether you are visiting the park, reading a book, or even walking to the store. Your child may also delight you with spontaneous outbursts of affection, disarming you with her endearing hugs, irresistible smiles, or infectious laughter; while you, in turn, can respond in an equally spontaneous way.

FIT FOR FUN
Humor and a sense of fun are vital qualities to have when spending some family time with a toddler..

Toddler characteristics

It is important not to confuse any family characteristics or potential personality traits with challenging toddler attributes. A stubborn or argumentative streak in a two-year-old is a typical form of behavior for a child of this age, and is not necessarily setting up key character traits for later life. Even so, it can sometimes be challenging to live with a two-year-old child who just doesn't want you to put her shoes on!

Accentuating the positive

Your child saying "No" is a reflection of her growing sense of self, which is positive and important – her way of learning what it means to be an independent person. While it may sometimes seem at this stage as if your child's favorite pastime is saying "no," it may be because this is one of the words she hears most from the grown-ups around her! It helps to think about reducing the number of times you have to say "no" to your child: rephrase some of your answers using humor, or give her a gentle challenge: "Can you put your hat on before I open my eyes?" This is a good time to reinforce any positive behavior with praise, and to start offering your child simple choices from two options.

Throughout this period, your child needs your guidance, reassurance, and unconditional love. It's not easy, and can sometimes bring out the two-year-old in the best of us! So remember which one of you is the adult and retain your sense of balance as you make this journey from toddler to preschooler together.

About this book

During this year of enormous and exciting change in your child's young life, your support, encouragement, and love can do more than anything else to help her blossom. Understanding how your child develops is essential to helping you tune into her needs and give her what is best for her.

Section 1

The first half of this book tells you about how your child's development will affect both her physical and her emotional needs. For example, your child still needs lots of opportunities to use her body to become physically competent, but she also needs to balance this level of activity with enough restorative sleep to allow her to recharge those batteries.

Being one step ahead in terms of knowing what to expect from your child will help you understand her so that you can respond in the best and most effective way possible. And being able to meet her needs in this way will not only help her feel loved and valued, but boost your confidence as a parent, too.

Section 2

The second half of this book contains information about how and when your child is likely to reach each new milestone. Although the information is organized month by month, it's important to remember that the timescale for every child is flexible. All children develop at different rates, and your child will progress in her own time at the speed that's right for her.

However, a certain amount of growth and development has to take place before each new skill can be acquired. So, for instance, don't expect your child to be able to manage her own buttons as she dresses herself until she has had time to try various activities and develop her skills of manual dexterity.

There are lots of practical things you can do to try to encourage your child along the way, and this section includes some ideas for games and activities that you can play with her. Giving your child the right kind of stimulation at just the right time will begin to build her confidence and self-esteem, and help give her the best possible start in life.

Family life

As a family, you have probably now settled into more of a predictable pattern and adapted to the emotional, physical, and perhaps financial changes that come with having children. Your toddler still has many new changes to adapt to and needs time and encouragement to learn how to handle them.

Parental responsibility

The enormity of being responsible for another life entails a very steep learning curve for most parents. Family life at the beginning of your child's third year should be settling into a routine and, as adults adapt to their individual and joint roles as parents this time together can become amazingly rewarding.

Family relationships

Whether your child is an only child, has recently been joined by a new brother or a sister, or has older siblings or stepsiblings, relationships with other members of the extended family are all-important for enriching your child's life: although his bond to you as parents is a primary relationship based on unconditional love, it's important for your child to have alternative sources of affection from people other than his parents. For example, he may be developing a particularly close relationship with relatives such as grandparents, or he may have a close bond with a caregiver or baby-sitter, which can be encouraged and supported by you.

The growing family

Every family is built upon different personalities and situations. A change in circumstances may occur for the first time in your child's life when a brother or sister is

born. Your child's reaction to this new arrival will probably depend on a variety of things:

- his individual personality and temperament
- your family's particular circumstances
- the age gap between siblings
- how the situation is presented to him.

While your child may express no jealousy or rivalry toward a new sibling at first, he may find the situation becomes increasingly difficult as his sibling grows older and is more likely to interfere with his toys or games. Since there is no perfect age gap between two children, it all depends on the children concerned – their response cannot be guaranteed, whatever their ages!

Sibling rivalry

At this age, children are likely to express extreme love or hate for a new arrival – often within the space of the same hour! And, while some children may adapt easily and happily with no concern for the new arrival's apparent imposition, others can feel very threatened by this new change.

The skill as a parent is to know when to intervene or not. It is important to find time to really listen and respond to the concerns of each child, and to try to meet each of their needs while balancing what's best for the family as a whole. While children at the age of two may sometimes appear desperate to be independent, they do still demand – quite reasonably – a lot of time and individual attention. At the same time, it is also worth emphasizing to your toddler that he or she now has a special, exciting new role as an older brother or sister.

Special times

Try to minimize the possibility of sibling rivalry by ensuring individual time and attention for a period every day with your toddler. You may feel as if whatever you give is never enough, but you can feel reassured that if your two-year-old knows he always has some definite one-to-one time together that can be relied upon without interruption from the baby, this will make a big, positive difference to him. Choose something to do together that a baby couldn't possibly join in with to increase the sense of importance of this precious time together.

NEW ADDITIONS
Taking on the role of older brother can be an exciting time for your toddler, as well as being an uncertain period of great change. Give him time to adjust, and be sure to spend time alone together.

Twins and triplets

With such advanced reproductive technologies now available, the incidence of twins and triplets is increasing. Twins and triplets form their own unique relationships with one another, but their needs as individual children are still very important, and can sometimes present unique demands on parents. If you feel that you need extra support, organizations such as NOMOTC (*below*) can provide you with practical advice to enable you to have the chance to spend some one-to-one time with each child and also with your partner.

Useful websites
www.nomotc.org
www.multiples.about.com
www.twiniality.com

Social & behavioral development

At this age your child is still centered on herself and her own needs, seeing the world almost exclusively from her point of view. This works to her advantage in some ways as she focuses on practicing her skills and abilities.

Learning to share

At this age your child is still very self-focused, and this is fairly typical behavior for her age group. She isn't being selfish if she behaves in a possessive or ungenerous way, but if she can't yet grasp why she should share what she knows is hers, it can sometimes make it difficult for her to be able to interact, or share toys and activities, with other children of a similar age and at the same stage of development. You will want to encourage her to think about other people, of course, but it is not until a child is five years old or more that she can demonstrate any unsolicited or sincere concern for someone else's needs.

Nurturing generosity

Attempting to influence the behavior of a child of this age by asking her to consider others doesn't have much of an impact since she genuinely can't yet empathize. Asking her to consider how she would feel if someone pushed her – as she has just done to another child – won't work. Keep it simple and reinforce the message, "We don't push other people."

  This doesn't mean you shouldn't have conversations about feelings at another time, but when managing anti-social behavior just insist that she doesn't do it. Also be sure that you always acknowledge and praise any kind and thoughtful behavior when it arises spontaneously, thereby reinforcing what your child is beginning to learn for herself about being social.

Preschool groups

Learning to be socially well adapted takes time, practice, and ultimately self-motivation; wanting to behave well to please you, rather than because you have to tell her,

Acquiring social skills

Most of what children learn about respecting other people's feelings is acquired through example and by observing others. If your child is treated with fairness and consideration, and then sees this repeated in the extended family and wider community, she will, in time, begin to understand what it means to be socially well adapted.

  Likewise, in spite of her typical toddler attributes of self-focus and possessiveness, it is important to encourage your child to mix with other children to help her social development. For instance, if an older child who has already learned to be more thoughtful, considerate, and tolerant, plays with your child, she can in turn learn from the example of the older child.

makes it much easier for your child to achieve. This is why meeting with other similarly aged children, perhaps at some sort of structured preschool group, can really help. Your child will gradually learn what is expected of her and of other children both from you and from the other adults outside of her family.

Other social skills

As your child begins to make this move out of the secure confines of her immediate family unit and into the wider world, she needs to become aware of other necessary social skills such as learning how to listen and cooperate. The primary way she learns how to do this is by example:

• how she is treated will in turn influence how she treats others

• if she is listened to when she speaks, she will learn to listen to others

• if she feels secure in her place, she won't have to fight so hard to be acknowledged.

If a child is insecure about how she fits into a larger group, she needs reassurance and positive attention so that she doesn't feel the need to be demanding or inconsiderate of others. Children of this age are still very self-focused, striving to satisfy their own needs even if it isn't always socially acceptable.

Changes in behavior

Social development is seldom a smooth progression, and all children can behave seemingly out of character on occasion. Whether it is in response to a specific incident, because your child isn't feeling well, or sometimes for no apparent reason, the fact is that it is completely in character for a child of this age sometimes to be unpredictable in her behavior.

Emotional development

At this stage, you will be increasingly aware of your child's emotional development. It is typical of this age group that a child will swing through a multitude of different emotions during the course of just one day. One minute your child may be insisting on doing things his way and refusing to do as you ask; the next minute he is clinging to your legs, refusing to let you move an inch without him.

Emotional inexperience

All young children show through their behavior what they can't express in words. This may be because they don't yet have the language skills, or haven't previously experienced the emotion, so they don't actually know what they are expressing.

For example, if there has been no previous reason for, or experience of, jealousy when a new baby arrives, it's hard for a young child to understand just what he feels. This can make him act quite aggressively as a result. Therefore small children are dependent on the loving adults around them, such as grandparents, who do have the emotional experience and thoughtfulness to reassure them and help them find a way to express their feelings.

Explaining emotions

It can also be hard for a child to explain that he feels angry at having to share his toys, for example, because he doesn't understand that they will be returned to him. He may not know what emotion he is feeling, since he might not have had much to get angry about before now.

In this situation it helps to let your child know that you understand how he is feeling by trying to put the situation into understandable language for him. Keep it

simple but say something reaffirming: "You seem to be feeling angry about Sam using your crayons. I know that sometimes it's hard to share, but don't worry. I will make sure that Sam takes care of them and gives them back to you when he has finished his drawing."

Feelings matter

Showing your child that you understand, and can help voice his fears for him, may take the heat out of the situation. This is much more effective than telling him not to be so silly and ungenerous, which implies that his feelings don't matter and may, in time, prevent the development of a healthy sense of self-esteem. If you show him that you care about how he is feeling, he can understand that his emotions – and by extension himself – matter to you, and that you are there to help him.

Showing affection and pleasure

By the same token, it is also important to identify and talk about positive feelings with your child, such as acknowledging the pleasure he obviously displays when

he sees a grandparent, or explaining to him how much you enjoy the quick hugs and kisses he may impulsively give you from time to time. It all helps him to understand better the different range of emotions he instinctively displays.

Parenting skills

Your child can gradually begin to learn from you how to manage his emotions:

- begin by acknowledging to your child which emotion he might be feeling
- give him a sense of security by telling him that you understand why he feels like this
- explain to him what is and isn't acceptable behavior
- distract his attention by encouraging him to move away and play another game with you
- get some paper and pens and suggest that you draw a picture for him of how he might be feeling – or show him different pictures of happy, sad, or cross faces – which may help him to refocus in a more positive way
- remain patient. Don't forget that how you act toward your child will have a big impact on how he learns to deal with his emotions.

Intense emotions

It is worth remembering that experiencing some intense emotions is often more than your child can handle, so don't get cross with him if he doesn't appear to respond to your efforts to help him or to distract his attention.

Remind yourself that the reason he is able to express his feelings with you is because he feels secure enough to do so. What he needs at this point is to know that you can understand his feelings, even if he can't. This feeling of reassurance will gradually give him confidence that if his emotions don't overwhelm you then they are manageable, and that eventually he will be able to manage them for himself.

Coping with shyness

Trying to determine whether your child has an inborn shyness or is just displaying typical toddler tendencies can be difficult. Always accept his shyness rather than dismiss it, and tell him that you understand how he is feeling. Keep encouraging him and avoid situations where he might attract undue attention — always being late for nursery school, for example. If he needs your physical reassurance to begin playing alongside other children, stay only as long as necessary; once he feels comfortable, tell him that you are going to sit down. You may like to try role-playing games with his toys or teddy bears to help him understand that other children and adults may also feel shy.

Creating secure limits

Your role as a parent includes creating a sense of security by setting secure limits, but your child's "job" in many ways is to test them! Exploration is key to how your child learns about her world, and that means investigating everything: her physical abilities, her emotions, and exactly what you will or won't allow her to do.

Figuring out the limits

Part of the way your child learns about her environment, and the people she shares it with, is through the direct result of many of her actions. By exploring the secure limits you set, a small child will work out what is and isn't permissible in her family, and by extension the wider world outside her family. If you demonstrate the rules of society – not hurting other people, for example – your child will learn from the people she lives with that she is loved and protected. Praising your two-year-old,

distracting her, and helping her to avoid confrontations are also valuable lessons for her to learn. Children who have been brought up in a permissive way without limits may find it difficult to learn how to behave outside the immediate family.

Making your child feel secure

Setting limits is important because it makes small children feel secure; if a child gets out of her depth it can sometimes be an overwhelming experience. There are several different ways you can help your child to know what to expect:

- praise and encourage any good behavior
- let her know in a loving way which behavior is acceptable, and which isn't allowed. This provides her with a sense of security if, for example, she knows that hitting another person is off limits
- decide which limits are absolute in your family and trying to be consistent with these. For example, that food is eaten only sitting at the table, or that only a grown-up can touch the video player
- avoid confrontation by distracting her with a toy, or inject a sense of humor into the situation, rather than repeatedly telling your child not to do something
- reinforce the message, since small children have limited memories.

Learning to be independent

Your child will not only explore the limits you have set, she will also test her own limits — physically, emotionally, and intellectually. This is part of her attempt to become more independent of you, trying things out on her own while still needing your support and guidance. Getting the balance right can be tricky: some days your child will manage quite well with a simple task, but other days — perhaps if she is tired or slightly sick — it may be beyond her. This constant fluctuation between a child who is managing well and one who needs support and reassurance (one minute rejecting your help and the next moment feeling clingy) is one of the characteristics of this age group and is what makes parenting such an intriguing challenge!

Curious explorers

Depending on their personality, some children accept limits more easily while others are avid explorers whose curiosity often overcomes them. But children at this age aren't being bad, or particularly "naughty." Even when your child knows that something will not please you, she is sometimes incapable of overcoming the urge to try it out, so great is her inclination to see what your reaction will be. This is evidence of how important you and your reaction are to her.

If you can't ignore such attention-seeking behavior, focus on what your child has done, expressing your displeasure at her actions, rather than at her. Make it clear that deliberately spilling her drink is unacceptable and can have consequences: she may have to help clean it up, or not get a refill, for example. A child's persistence may even be a way of expressing a confidence in her growing ability to accomplish something. If some of the safe limits you have set are age- or ability-related, you may need to adjust them over time.

Managing the situation

There are several ways you can help your child to learn to accept limits that will benefit her development.

• **Limit the number of ways she can say "no."** Phrase a question so that you don't offer a choice if there isn't one: if it is time to go home, don't ask her if she'd like to go, merely state that it's time to leave in five minutes

• **Be consistent.** By making sure things happen when you say they will your child will learn that there is no point in making a fuss

• **Make a game of it.** For example, see if your child can wash her hands before you finish setting the table

• **Reassure yourself** that, as your child grows, so will her ability to understand why things happen as they do – that you put her coat on when it rains to protect and care for her, not to restrict her.

Repeating the praise

If your child attempts something beyond her capabilities and doesn't succeed, keep praising her and giving her the guidance and support that she needs to realize that mistakes are in fact a creative opportunity to learn how to solve problems. If we give children the message that only successful accomplishments are worthwhile, and don't focus on the effort and care that goes into them, then they may put off trying to extend their abilities or testing their limits.

Discipline

Discipline is about teaching your child what you expect of him by encouraging him and setting an example. It also helps him learn, in time, to manage his own behavior without always referring to you. Discipline is not about punishment.

Why toddlers need discipline

Teaching your child to manage his own behavior is the beginning of self-discipline, something we all need to learn in order to function confidently in society and alongside other people. Self-discipline not only enables us to judge what is appropriate behavior in a certain situation, it also helps us complete tasks for ourselves, concentrate on activities, deal with minor frustrations, and work toward the sort of self-motivation and self-esteem that makes us competent and independent people. Learning how to do all of this has to begin at an early age in order to instill a basic understanding of what is acceptable, and what is not.

Positive parenting

Understanding your child's behavior is a vital part of positive parenting. Teach him by showing your love and encouragement, and through your own example. Feeling secure in the love and care of a parent frees up a young child's emotional life so that he can concentrate on the positive aspects of being a child, playing and learning in preparation for the time he can begin to take responsibility for himself.

LEARNING TO BE RESPONSIBLE
Give your child your attention and praise when she does what you ask of her, such as bringing her shoes to you. If you explain to her how helpful her behavior is, she will probably want to do it again.

Appropriate parenting skills

When it comes to managing your child's behavior, the skill of parenting is to go for balance.

- **Give choices.** Allow your child the freedom, within the parameters you set, to make choices that reflect his growing sense of independence. For example, if you ask him what he'd like to eat, limit it to an either/or choice to make his decision manageable.
- **Avoid overcontrolling your child.** For example, don't hover over him in the expectation that he will play up to you.
- **Acknowledge positive behavior** and gently correct unacceptable behavior. When he chooses to behave well or share a toy, congratulate him on his ability or contribution – it will make him want to please you again.
- **Establish a routine.** This will help him learn to feel much more secure.

Learning by example

As your child progresses through his third year, you can expect him to have a growing understanding of what you ask of him. Children at this age have limited memories, but constant gentle reminders will finally pay off. He will know that there are things that he can't have to play with because they belong to someone else, or they aren't for playing with because they are easily broken. He will also hear you explain about learning to respect other people's feelings and property, and it is only fair that he, in turn, receives the same consideration. By having the same courtesy extended to him, he learns to treat other people and their possessions well; as is so often the case, children learn this skill by example.

Consistent teaching

At this age, help your child to understand by example and by giving him explanations. His improving language development and ability to understand allow you to

Rewarding good behavior

Discipline and self-discipline ultimately help instill a sense of self-confidence in your child, as does your positive reinforcement of his good behavior.

Make sure that you always notice when your child has behaved well, or successfully managed to complete something you have asked him to do. Let him see your appreciation for what he has done, rather than taking such an achievement for granted. Be specific with your praise, too. Tell him how pleased you are that he helped you clear up his toys, for example, or how quiet he tried to be while you finished talking on the telephone.

If he receives lots of positive praise – and hugs if he enjoys them – for his good behavior, then your child will soon learn that he won't have to resort to behaving badly in order to get your attention.

talk through with him why you would like him to do something in a certain way. Follow through that explanation by checking that your child actually does what you request, or help him in the most appropriate way. For instance, if you have asked your child specifically not to touch something, then you must ensure that he doesn't. Remove him from the vicinity, take the object away from him, or prevent him from reaching it. If he expresses his displeasure with a display of negative emotions, distract him or calmly ignore him until it passes.

You also need to remember to be consistent. Don't confuse your child by insisting that all his toys need to be put away before dinnertime one day and then overlooking it the next, or encouraging him to try undressing himself on his own one night and then not having the patience to let him try again. If you do need to make an exception, tell him why. It will be easier for him in the long run if you are consistent; otherwise, he will have to test you out on everything every time, which is exhausting for both of you.

Tantrums

This is a very self-focused time for your child, and she is preoccupied with her own wants and desires. It is also common for a toddler to express her feelings volubly and physically if she feels frustrated or thwarted in some way.

What are tantrums?

Two-year-olds are renowned for their tantrums, but in practice this depends more on a child's individual personality and temperament, and whether or not she is developmentally able to manage her emotions. It can also depend on whether a child has learned early on that having a tantrum assures her of her parent's or her baby-sitter's attention; she may now use tantrums as an emotional ploy to attract further attention.

Tantrums occur when your child is overwhelmed by her feelings, which are usually born out of frustration. When people don't understand what she might be trying to say, or if she tries do to something beyond her capabilities and fails, it can be very frustrating. Inconsistency can also confuse a small child – such as being given candy on one trip to the supermarket and then being denied that special treat on subsequent shopping trips.

Equally difficult for a two-year-old is managing to calm herself down once she's reached a high level of distress because she hasn't yet learned how. It can all be rather bewildering and overwhelming at times, and that is when a child really needs an adult's help.

Identifying tantrum triggers

Emotional outbursts are often an expression of frustration, although some children react to distress and fear in a similar way. Learning how to manage frustrations and to see difficulties in context as they arise is an acquired skill and your child will need your gentle guidance to find out how. The older and bigger your child gets, the more difficult tantrums are to manage, so there are a variety of approaches that are worth considering to try to prevent tantrums from becoming a regular occurrence.

● **Look out for triggers that you know from experience can lead to a tantrum.** Does your child find it difficult to manage new things toward the end of the day, or to

A passing phase

Perhaps the most important thing to remember about your child having tantrums is that they are a phase and they will pass, so make sure that you applaud and reward your child's good behavior, rather than take it for granted.

Not always saying "No" to something can also help. If your child's request for something is made at an inappropriate time, instead of saying "No" you can say, "That's a good idea, shall we get some for later?" or "Yes, we will do that but after we have done this." In this way you can demonstrate that you have heard your child's suggestion, taken it on board, and allowed her contribution to be validated – all of which makes her feel good about herself, and valued. When children feel secure they tend to act up less and so have tantrums less frequently.

share toys? Is her inability to do things beyond her capabilities overwhelming her confidence? Avoid end-of-day demands, and find toys ahead of time that she has agreed to share, putting the rest away for now.

● **Is she tired, thirsty, hungry, or sick?** Don't expect too much from your child under these conditions. Make sure that her physical needs are met so that your child is less distracted and can focus more easily on what is required of her emotionally.

● **Acknowledge the situation from her point of view.** It takes a certain amount of maturity, not available to your child yet, to cope when under stress. Even the most apparently inconsequential things can set off a child who is feeling vulnerable. The fact that her cookie is broken may mean little to you, but to your inconsolable child it is the end of the world – respect her feelings.

● **Sometimes a tantrum is inevitable.** Some children at this age actually seem to need an emotional blowout in order to let go. If this happens to your child and it is too late for you to try diversionary tactics, go into management mode. Make sure your child is safe, then stand nearby without focusing on her, and reassure her that you will be there when she calms down. You should then let the issue pass.

Feeling reassured

Many children find having a tantrum quite frightening and will need your reassurance. Keep encouraging your child to do those things that she is capable of with enjoyment, working toward greater challenges so that her confidence grows and her self esteem increases.

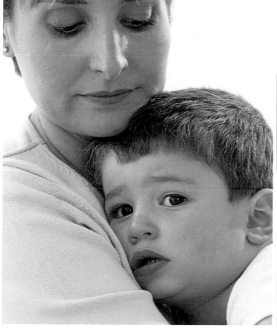

AVOIDING A CRISIS
Because you love your child, and his distress is something you'd like to avoid, giving him a reassuring cuddle and using humor may help to diffuse a difficult crisis. Or try distracting his attention by pointing out something of interest and steering the conversation in that direction.

Health & developmental checkup

A health checkup undertaken some time during your child's third year includes a physical exam to ensure that his growth is in line with what has been previously charted. A hearing check, eye test, and developmental check are also routine.

A review of your child's health in his third year is a time to monitor his health, as well as his growth and development, and to make sure that there are no problems with his hearing or vision. If there are problems with his ability to see or hear, they need to be addressed and rectified as soon as possible. A healthcare professional will also listen to your child's heart and lungs, and you will be asked about which infectious diseases and other illnesses your child has had and about any recurrent problems such as ear infections. You will probably also be asked about what provision you have made for your child's dental care, too. This health checkup may include a blood test for hemoglobin, or lead levels, if any problem is suspected. This is quite a common procedure in the United States. A urine test, though not routine, may also be required.

Fine motor skills

Your child's hand movements are becoming more precise. Turning the pages of a book one at a time, holding a pencil correctly, and using a cup with one hand are all examples of the greater dexterity she is now developing at this age.

One thing that has benefited this phase in her development is her ability to focus on one activity for longer periods. This in turn gives her the ability and concentration to develop more creative tendencies, such as beginning to draw using her imagination and observation skills.

HOW TO DRAW
Your child's hand–eye coordination is becoming more precise.

General questions

The healthcare professional will ask questions about your child's behavior and eating and sleep habits. This is an opportunity for you to ask for information and guidance about anything that concerns you, and discuss any forthcoming changes in your child's life, for example toilet training, the birth of a sibling, or sorting out child care.

Percentile charts

Routinely measuring the height and weight of your child and charting it on a percentile chart from birth, will give you a good indication of his progress. The percentile divisions relate to the percentage of children of the same age that are within a specific growth band. The 50th centile marks the average, which means that, if you take 100 babies, 50 will be heavier and taller than the 50th line (above it) and 50 will be lighter and smaller (below it). The majority of children, 82 percent, fall between the 9th and 91st centile. The charts are in two forms, one for boys and one for girls, since girls tend to be physically smaller than boys from birth. Children grow in fits and starts, so their progress doesn't necessarily follow the smooth curve of the chart. If your child is healthy and active, he is probably growing well and there is normally some fluctuation along the way, but if your child shows a big divergence between his height and weight – for example, 60 percent height but 95 percent weight – you should consult a healthcare professional.

Social trends

There has been an increase in the average height throughout the developed world. This is known as the "secular trend." For example, five-year-olds in Britain today are on average 3in (7–8cm) taller than 100 years ago. The "mid-parental height" may give an indication of what height children will be: add the mother's and father's heights in inches together, divide by two, and

add three to work out your son's likely height at 18 years old. To calculate a girl's height, you should subtract three from the final result because girls tend to fluctuate by 3½in (8.5cm) either way of their mid-parental height.

Finally, the healthcare professional will probably check that your child has received all the relevant routine immunizations needed to protect him from serious illnesses, and that his immunization schedule is up-to-date – something that is often obligatory prior to school entry in the US.

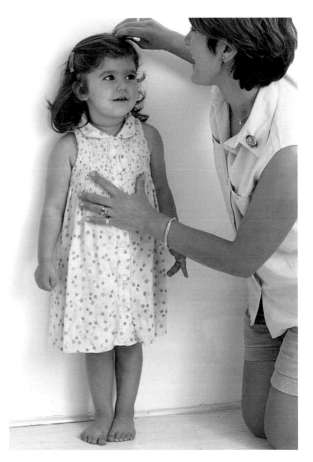

CHECKING HEIGHT
Children tend to reflect the height of their parents: tall parents often have tall children. If you wish, you can work out roughly how tall your child will be when fully grown by using the "mid-parental height" described above).

Toilet training

Toilet training is only possible when your child is able to control the muscles of her anus and bladder. These muscles usually mature between 18 and 36 months, so it is generally recommended to start toilet training after she is at least two years old.

Picking the right time

Toilet training as a notion is a bit of a misnomer because you can't really train a child until she is physically ready. However, once she shows signs that she is capable developmentally and shows an emotional willingness, then the process should be a pretty straightforward one.

It is worth having the potty visible and available in the bathroom for some months prior to the start of formal training to allow your child the chance to get used to sitting on it and even occasionally managing to use it successfully, which is a good basis from which to start.

Nighttime training

Even when your child is happily out of diapers during the day, she may still need a diaper for nap times during the day or at nighttime. You can introduce the idea of going without a diaper by ensuring that she uses the potty before going to sleep. She may well have a dry diaper as a consequence, especially when she wakes from her daytime nap.

If she is waking in the morning regularly with a dry diaper, then you can probably try going without one at night. Make sure you have a protective waterproof cover for the mattress of her bed, and check that there is enough light at night for her to be able to manage to use the potty or toilet – probably with your help at first, and then on her own as she grows older and becomes more experienced.

In addition to developing the necessary muscle control, your child may be showing signs of other skills:
- is she beginning to try to remove her pants without your help? It may help focus her attention by involving her in choosing some new underwear to buy.
- is she able to sit down on a potty and get up easily?
- does she know when she has the urge to go, and can she tell you?

All these things make it easier for her to be successful when the time comes. In the past, to escape the tyranny of endlessly washing cloth diapers, toilet training began at a much earlier age and involved a lot of time sitting on potties waiting for things to happen. There was a certain amount of success, but this depended on parents making a potty available at the right time rather than the babies being able to control their bladders and bowels. Studies show that many children who begin toilet training before 18 months old aren't completely trained until after the age of four, whereas those who started at around age two were completely trained before their third birthday.

Start looking for signals of your child being ready to try managing without a diaper:
- has she seen you or other family members use the toilet?
- is she aware of urinating or having a bowel movement, even when wearing a diaper, and tells you?
- does she sit on and try to use the potty, perhaps before her bath in the evening?

Once you have some evidence that your child has an idea of what is going to be required of her once she goes without diapers, you can consider taking the next step. Avoid a time when your child is having to cope with other changes in her life, such as a house move, a new baby, or some other adaptation she needs to make. It will be easier for her, and you, without additional stresses to cope with.

FAMILIARITY
Let your child become familiar with sitting on a potty so that she'll be happy to use it properly when the right time comes.

Practical concerns

Make sure you have a potty that is comfortable to sit on, and for boys it's helpful to have one that has a higher splashguard at the front than at the back. You will also have to help your son understand that his penis will need to point inside the potty to be successful. It's easy for a boy to sit down quickly without checking and find he is going outside the potty, which is very dispiriting!

Once you think your child is ready, explain that without diapers she will need to use the potty. Because modern diapers are designed to prevent any feelings of wetness, it may not be until she is diaper-free that she can really make the connection between wanting to urinate, and what it feels like. You may have to tolerate several "accidents" or near misses before she learns this.

Once you replace diapers with pants, you may want to use thicker, terry-cotton training pants for a while. These can still feel rather like diapers, so you may have more success moving straight to ordinary underwear.

Getting into a routine

You will also need to give your child regular reminders that she might like to use the potty. Having asked her, don't sit her on the potty unless she says yes; otherwise, she won't make the connection for herself. Sometimes she may say no, and two minutes later realize she does feel the urge to go, which is better than relying on you to tell her. Some accidents are inevitable, but if your child is ready to manage without a diaper these should number very few. Work on the principle of praising her efforts and successes, and, if accidents do occur, gently remind her that this is what the potty is for, change her, and make no fuss. Reacting negatively may make her resentful and less inclined to try again.

Finally, it's worth remembering that every child develops at a different rate and will be trained at their own pace. Patience is key.

Sleep issues

Active, busy children who are growing rapidly still need lots of sleep to restore and refresh them. At this age, you can anticipate the sleep needs of a toddler to be between nine and 13 hours during a 24-hour period.

Physical benefits

Not only is sleep important to young children in order for them to have the energy they need to enjoy life, it is also during deep sleep that pituitary growth hormone is secreted in the brain. Therefore cell growth and cell renewal and repair in young children mainly occurs during sleep. It is also worth noting that children don't grow continuously but in spurts. During a growth spurt, which can happen virtually overnight, your child may need extra sleep. Inadequate sleep and wakeful nights can be detrimental to long-term health, as well as creating sleep patterns that become habits, so if your child is still a poor sleeper, try to rectify this now (*see also box on night waking, p.26*).

Family needs

Depending on each child's individual needs, you may find your child requires just one good nap during the day now, while some children will still need two naps. It also partly depends on your family routine: if you want your child to be happily awake until later in the evening so that you can all eat together after work, he probably needs at least one good nap of at least two hours later during the day to manage this good-humoredly. If, however, it is better for his schedule and his sleep needs for him to be in bed by seven o'clock every night, then a shorter nap earlier in the day will probably suit him better.

Checking sleep patterns

Although children vary in their sleep needs, your rule of thumb should be how your child manages during the day. If he is happy and showing no real behavioral difficulties, even though he only sleeps for eight hours at night with a short daytime nap, that's fine. But if he is consistently grumpy, finds socializing difficult, and is argumentative over everything, review his sleep patterns. No one manages well when they haven't had enough sleep, and it may be that increasing the amount of sleep he gets will help considerably. In addition, remember that during times of emotional and physical demand – sickness experiences such a new babysitting arrangement, family stress, even holidays – your child may need more sleep to compensate. New experiences can be very stimulating, even overstimulating, and, depending on your child's temperament, you may need to balance them with extra sleep to help him recuperate in between.

A busy social life

During this third year, your child's life has probably become quite busy. It may be more social, perhaps with regular play group sessions or childcare arrangements away from home. All of this is very stimulating, which is positive, but which can also be quite physically and emotionally demanding. If he doesn't want to sleep, schedule opportunities to recharge those batteries with some quiet times. Learning how to have a quiet time by

himself, perhaps with a book or a puzzle, is an important ability to acquire as your child matures. This won't be for a long stretch of time to begin with, but it does introduce to your child the idea of being self-motivated and self-sufficient.

Bedtime routines

With all his emerging independence and growing abilities, you may find that your child begins to present some resistance to going to bed. Depending on how your family life is organized, there may be some reason that needs to be acknowledged:

● is there a new baby who goes to bed at the same time as he does, without allowing any time for a one-to-one storytelling session?

● is he so overstimulated that he is unable to go to sleep easily?

● does his bedtime coincide now with a parent's return from work, with whom he wants to spend some time? It's always worth looking at what might be the cause of change in a child's behavior, and meet your child's needs as these behaviors change.

Winding down

After the last meal of your child's day, allow some time for a quiet play before having a bath or shower and preparing for bed. The benefit of a routine is that the familiarity of events, which draw toward the inevitably of bedtime, contribute to a feeling of enjoyment about the end of the day. Finish the routine with one last milky drink if your child enjoys it, brushing of teeth, story and cuddle, and then bed. A predictable sequence of events may help your child realize that it's not worth making a fuss about something that will happen whatever he does.

Night waking

For some children, bedtimes and night waking are a problem, however, trying to ensure that bedtime is a peaceful routine may help to reduce the incidence of night waking. If a child is able to fall asleep peacefully alone, when he surfaces in his sleep or wakes briefly in the night he should be able to go back to sleep by himself without any need for intervention from you.

Babies have a sleep cycle moving from light to deep sleep of around 50 minutes, in contrast to an adult's sleep cycle of around 90 minutes. This means that small children move through light and deep periods of sleep more often, and if they haven't learned to settle alone the possibility for night waking is increased. Babies and toddlers who are perpetually assisted by rocking or feeding will have difficulty learning to go to sleep alone and this can become a habit. If this habit becomes entrenched, it means that a child can't be fully independent about going to sleep.

A consistent bedtime routine helps create a sense of security, which enables him to "let go" and fall asleep. Allowing your child to learn to go to sleep on his own is a positive step towards his growing independence.

If your child finds it difficult to relax, a massage can be a beneficial way to help him calm down. Use a specially formulated baby oil or lotion to massage his feet as he lies on his bed, the floor, or the sofa, or keep him warm after his bath and give him a soothing tummy rub. Gently massaging the shoulders helps release tension, and many children love having their scalps massaged, although you don't need to use oil. You could also try rhythmically brushing his hair, keeping it gentle. It partly depends on your child's preference, but if massage has been a part of your previous baby care routine reintroduce it now. For others it may be a new experience and take some adjusting to, so keep it short and light.

Getting to sleep

Some children will fall asleep straight away; others take a while to drift off. Reassure your child that lying in bed, perhaps thinking about positive things that happened during the day, is good, and that falling asleep will follow. It may be that listening to a peaceful piece of music, or just being aware of the family moving around close by, is more reassuring than silence. However, be quite firm that, once bedtime arrives, getting up again is not an option. Say you will pop back in 10 minutes to check on him and that he is not to get out of bed, but do remember to go back since he may deliberately stay awake. When you go back there is no need to do anything except say, "Sleep well." Lengthen the time before you next check on him and you should find he is asleep!

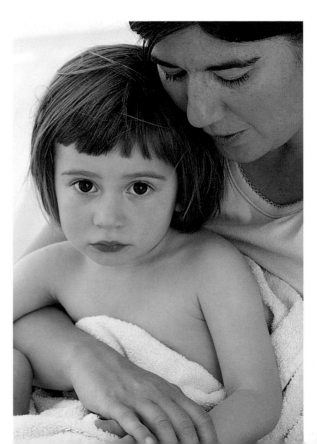

Changing nighttime habits

Moving into his own bed will delight most toddlers. If your child needs time to make the transition to a bed, try putting the bed up before removing his crib, assuming there's room. Let him put his teddy bear in the bed or take his daytime naps there until he's happy to spend all night in it. It is also important to put up guard rails on the sides of the bed so that he can't fall out at night.

Now that your child is physically able to get out of bed, some new nighttime habits may arise! Getting into your bed in the night may begin on a regular basis. Lots of families tolerate this but it is at a price since everyone's sleep gets disrupted. Research shows that toddlers who sleep in bed with their parents tend to wake more often.

If it is a new habit, it may be linked to a recent event. Perhaps you nursed your child in your bed during a recent illness he had; though the illness has passed, his habit of being in your bed may not have. Maybe a new event has occurred – moving house or having another baby-sitter. Whatever the reason, give your child lots of time and attention during the day so that he doesn't feel the need to seek it during the night. Comfort him, but be firm about returning him to his own bed.

Bad dreams

Occasionally children have bad dreams, which usually occur during the second half of the night, when dreams are strongest. Dreams occur during REM (rapid eye movement) sleep, when the body is in such a state of deep muscle relaxation that movement is impossible. If dreams occur during the shift from REM to non-REM sleep, which can often be the case, your child may wake. If he is distressed, go to him immediately. He may fear returning to sleep, so stay with him awhile, reassuring him and check that he is not too hot or cold, but don't get him up. The occasional bad dream isn't significant if your child appears happy during the day, but it might make him anxious about going to sleep in case it recurs. Reassure him that his dreams can't hurt him and explain that everyone dreams. Check that he hasn't seen or heard anything inappropriate in a story or on television; some TV programs can be quite scary.

Nighttime accidents

When children move out of nighttime diapers they may become anxious about wetting the bed. Play this down, ensure there is a waterproof cover on the bed, and, if it becomes an issue, return to nighttime diapers for a while. Once he sees that his diaper is dry most mornings he will gain confidence. There is no point introducing anxiety at night for the sake of moving out of diapers.

Feeding routines

By now your child should be eating meals with the family, although you may want to adjust these occasionally to make them child-friendly and adapt some of your own eating habits to ensure that you provide your child with what is good for her.

Getting the right balance

Your child's diet should be healthy and balanced; keep in mind that the types of foods she eats now provide her with a blueprint for eating habits for the rest of her life.

Avoid fried foods that are heavy in saturated fats and additional salt and sugar, opting instead for steamed and grilled foods. Use fresh ingredients since processed foods are high in salt, sugars, and artificial flavorings. Children need protein for growth, carbohydrates and fats for

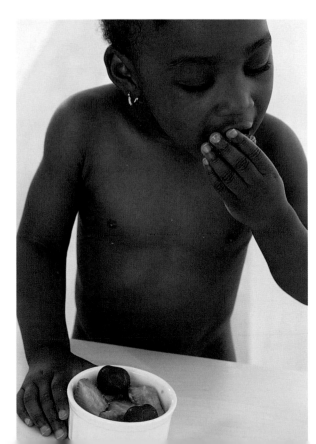

energy, and fruit and vegetables to supply vitamins and fiber, so choose foods from the four basic food groups:
- meat, fish, eggs, and other protein foods
- milk, cheese, yogurt, and other dairy products
- rice, cereals, potatoes, bread, pasta, and other carbohydrates
- fruits and vegetables.

Families who are vegetarian should be aware that milk and cheese also contain high sources of protein, as do soy and eggs. Large quantities of pulses and grains can be too bulky for children's stomachs; every mouthful needs to be as nutritious as possible. Egg yolk, spinach, and broccoli provide excellent sources of iron, and a vitamin and mineral supplement may also be beneficial.

Setting a good example

If you want your child to develop an appetite for fresh fruit and vegetables, set an example by eating plenty of these yourself. Don't expect your child to eat a banana if you snack on doughnuts or chocolate, or offer sweet treats (which promote sweet cravings and tooth decay) as rewards. Don't bargain with your child to encourage her to eat well; it could become a difficult habit to break.

Fluctuating appetites

Keep in mind that at this age your child's appetite may vary. Some days she will seem hungrier than on others, so it's sometimes useful to look at what she's eaten over a period of days rather than just one. Although she will benefit from a nutritious, well-balanced diet, she isn't growing as fast as she was and so may not always be quite as hungry.

What is useful is to offer foods that provide a nutritional combination – for example, a piece of cheese provides calcium and protein. This works well for children with a picky appetite: offer calorie- and protein-dense foods such as avocados, beans, whole milk, peanut butter (if you are certain that your child has no nut allergies), or cheese. It's possible to use foods that offer nutrition but with fewer calories for those children whose weight gain is too fast, such as fresh fruits and vegetables and wholegrain pastas (see also p.30).

Checking the sugar levels

You may want to think carefully about how much sugar is present in your child's diet. Often sugars are added by manufacturers to make processed foods more palatable to young children, for example, breakfast cereals already frosted with sugar. Sugar provides what is known as "empty calories," which have no nutritional value. An excessive sugar intake is also linked to the increased incidence of childhood obesity and diabetes.

Drinks

Water is the best and most refreshing drink to give to a thirsty child, so always offer this as a first choice, and at mealtimes. Tap water is perfectly safe for toddlers to drink, but mineral waters should not be given to young children because their mineral content could be too high in salts and other minerals.

If you filter your tap water, you must remember to change the filter regularly in accordance with the manufacturers' instructions. If your household system includes a water softener, you should ensure that your child drinks the water from the unsoftened water faucet only.

Brushing teeth

By two and half years old, your child should have all her first, or baby, teeth, including the second molars.

Regular teeth cleaning at least twice a day is essential to keep her teeth in good condition and prepare for the second teeth already developing in the gums. Supervise your child while she brushes since you will need to do some extra brushing for her, and don't let her use much toothpaste until she can spit it all out. Take her to the dentist for regular checkups: eight percent of two-year-olds have one or more cavities, increasing to nearly 60 percent by the age of three.

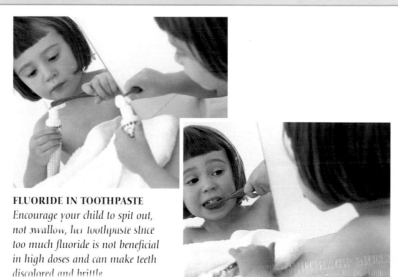

FLUORIDE IN TOOTHPASTE
Encourage your child to spit out, not swallow, her toothpaste since too much fluoride is not beneficial in high doses and can make teeth discolored and brittle.

After the age of two it is possible to give low-fat milk as a drink unless your child would still benefit from the calories in whole milk. Young children with small appetites but high-energy demands often need the additional calories provided by whole milk. In general, a low-fat diet isn't good for small children who have small appetites and are only capable of eating limited quantities of food; they need calorie-dense foods. Unless your child is on a calorie-controlled diet for some reason and is monitored by a pediatric dietitian, don't deliberately reduce her calorie intake.

It's all too easy to give your child sugar inadvertently via commercially prepared fruit drinks. Make sure you dilute these concentrates carefully, and use them only as an occasional treat to flavor water. Fresh fruit juices are also high in sugars and fruit acids that damage teeth, so these should be diluted as well. Avoid giving a child with a poor appetite large sugary drinks with meals. Drinking these will stop her from feeling hungry and prevent her from eating properly. The same applies to milky drinks: offer them at the end of a meal, or as a snack. If your child has between 16 to 32oz of milk (500–900ml) a day of milk as a drink or in cooked foods, all her calcium requirements for healthy bones will be met. But always try first to offer your child water as a drink with meals and to help quench her thirst.

Mealtimes

Eating together is one of the great social pleasures of family life, but it's all too easy to become a family who eats separately in shifts or in front of the television. If you want your child to enjoy her food, let her participate in the preparation of meals and mealtimes herself, then create the family occasion that helps her develop the social skills that will eventually enable her to socialize in the wider world. Family meals provide an opportunity to learn by example about table manners and consideration for other people eating together. And, while you can't expect a toddler always to tolerate a lengthy three-course meal with adults, you can expect her to enjoy some of it and participate – such as helping to lay the table, or carrying a dish out to the kitchen.

Mealtime schedules

Listed below are examples of drinks, snacks, and meals from the four main food groups. Aim to give four small portions each of protein and calcium, two or more small portions each of vegetables and fruits, and six small portions of grains and carbohydrates through the day. This schedule should help children avoid snacking in between mealtimes.

Breakfast	Mid-am snack	Lunch	Mid-pm snack	Dinner	Bedtime
Cereal with milk	Fruit	Cheese sandwich	Fruit	Minced chicken, rice, and vegetables	Banana or a cracker (optional)
Fruit	Yogurt	Cracker	Cheese	Stewed fruit or fromage frais	Milk or water
Toast	Milk	Fruit or vegetables	Milk	Water	
Waffle or a pancake		Water			
Diluted juice					

At this age your child may express quite definite tastes in food and have numerous favorites. Build on these, offering variety where you can to keep meals suitable for all the family. In fact, your child may well opt to eat only a limited variety of foods as a gesture of independence. It sometimes helps to offer a choice between one or two items, rather than asking, "What would you like to eat?" Giving her a choice, albeit limited, helps her feel that she has some say in the matter. If you offer other substitutes, you create the possibility of endless choice, which can be confusing for many small children.

Mealtime manners

If you want your child to be able to behave well when you visit friends or relatives or eat out in restaurants, it's worthwhile giving her the ground rules at home. Sitting at the dinner table for long periods of time is difficult for small children, but impossible if they have never had experience of doing it at home. If mealtimes are enjoyable social occasions at home, then your child's anticipation is that this will be a similar experience wherever she eats. If she always eats in isolation, she won't experience being part of a group elsewhere.

Restaurant etiquette

It takes a bit of practice for small children to get used to eating out in restaurants, and the following points are worth keeping in mind.

● **Choose child-friendly places** that serve food without much of a wait.

● **Take a favorite book** or small toy with which your child can occupy herself if her interest in her food and surroundings starts to wane.

● **Avoid taking overly tired or hungry children** since they are unlikely to be able to cope well.

● **Stay relaxed and enjoy the experience** of eating out with your children. Many children respond well when they see the way other people behave in restaurants. If you praise your child for being grown up, she is more likely to meet your expectations and behave well

Language development

Two-year-olds can vary enormously in their language development. Some children are naturally talkative and may already be talking quite extensively, while others may still only be using single words.

Even children of the same intelligence can vary widely in their language development. This is due to a combination of a child's temperament and personality and the opportunities that are available to encourage and increase his language development.

More than just words

In some families, children and their parents or adult caregivers may rely on nonverbal communication, gestures, intonation, and a shared common knowledge of day-to-day life. The use of one word can be subtly changed by the use of intonation and even volume. A questioning tone will turn one word into a request – for example, "Drink?", to which you might reply, "Would you like a drink?" and receive the answer with a nod of "Drink." Parents and caregivers become familiar with a child's efforts to communicate, and help him learn by listening and replying, often reiterating the question to indicate his effort to communicate has been understood.

Expanding vocabulary

At the age of two your child will probably understand much of what you say to him. By contrast, his own vocabulary now averages around fifty words or more. This vocabulary is growing rapidly, and he will soon progress from one-word statements to two- or three-word phrases. This improving development of language in turn promotes an increased understanding of a great

Hearing

The ability to hear is a very important requirement to speech. Without being able to hear, it is impossible for a child to learn to talk, since spoken language is dependent on imitating vocal sounds in a way that gets you understood. The sooner any hearing problem is picked up, the better it is for the child and his development. Recurrent ear infections, and glue ear in particular, which causes intermittent deafness, can adversely affect your child's language development.

Even if your child can hear perfectly, he still needs to be able to distinguish different word sounds apart from the possible interference of background noise. There is a potential risk to young children's hearing from continuous loud music, for example, at a sporting event. It is very important that your child has lots of one-to-one communication without any audible distraction so that he gets the benefit of hearing clearly not only what is being said but also the sounds of words. This will enable him to copy what he hears accurately and will also train his brain to distinguish what sounds make up a word.

This will help him later on in life, too, when he starts to read and write and spell. So make sure that the television or the radio isn't constantly providing a background noise and turn it off completely unless you are actually listening to it or watching something. Your child isn't able to screen out noise as well as you can when he is trying to listen and he needs to hear your words clearly and precisely if he is to increase the range of vocabulary he uses.

deal more words. Experimentation also comes into play as children provide their own meaning when seeking to apply language correctly. For example, for a while the word "Daddy" may be applied to all men or the word "dog" to all four-legged animals.

If your child tries to tell you something and you continually misunderstand him, it can lead to a great deal of frustration on your child's part. Communication is key to avoiding this buildup of frustration and feeling of inability. The best way to deal with this is to try to work within your child's frame of reference — acknowledge that he is attempting to express himself and ask him to show you or repeat himself so that you can carefully work out what he is saying.

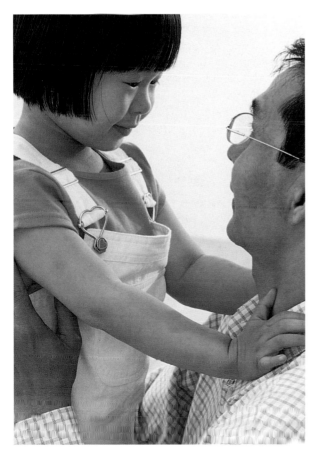

Building up language

The use of two-word sentences usually follows about six months after the first words, and meaning is often added by nonverbal gestures such as pointing, or activities that express meaning such as the urgency of pulling on your sleeve to get your attention. Two-word sentences include things like, "cup milk," "teddy gone," "car red," for example.

There is much you can do to help. Don't correct the mistakes naturally made when practicing language, but reiterate and reinforce what is said. So, with the previous examples, you might answer, "Would you like a cup of milk?", "Yes, the teddy has gone. He's fallen down," "That car is red, and this car is blue." As you build on whatever has engaged your child's attention, keep things simple and focus on the pleasure of communication.

Sometimes the verbal stimulation of older siblings may also encourage a toddler to build up his language sooner, and help him to focus on the pleasure he can gain from communicating with them.

Pronunciation

Reiterating what is said by repeating your child's words clearly and simply back to him also helps with his pronunciation. While it may sometimes sound very cute when a small child mispronounces a word, even if you can understand him, it is not helpful when he needs to be understood outside the immediate family. Persistent mispronunciation also creates problems when it comes to learning how to spell words. If your child can't hear and speak words clearly, he may have problems when he tries to write phonetically spelled words correctly.

Positive impact

The connection between language development and the ability to read and write later has been proved quite conclusively in research studies. You can help promote your child's language skills by spending short one-on-

one periods of time together at different points during the day – no longer than 10 to 15 minutes at a time – to explore a toy together, play or sing rhyming games, or look at a book without any background noise. Talking about an object or following a sung sequence or story can have an enormously positive impact. Children who have received this sort of input at this stage show a reading age almost 18 months ahead of their peer group by age seven.

The reason it makes such a difference is because after your child has learned the individual letters of the alphabet and their sounds, his ability to hear different letter sounds makes it easier to identify them when they are seen written down. The words cat and mat have a very distinctive ending sound of "at," but, because of the different letters at the beginning, two separate meanings. Distinguishing between letter sounds becomes even more important later when working out how to spell words.

Detecting problems

Since language development is so key to your child's intellectual progress, you will want to do all you can to encourage it and make sure there is nothing preventing it. Approximately one in every 10–15 children has problems with language comprehension or with the development of his speech.

Early detection and identification of a problem is important to ensure that language delay doesn't interfere with learning in other areas. If this is detected before school starts, the problems can be effectively addressed. Routine checkups at this stage include hearing and developmental checks to ensure that, if any problem is detected, a referral can be made for a more complete evaluation (see p.20). Even if it's a minor problem that can be easily remedied, the problem can escalate if it is not picked up.

Stuttering

Stuttering is thought to affect the speech of about four percent of preschoolers, but only one percent of the adult population, so it is often just a phase and is more common in younger siblings. Stuttering can occur when the physical mechanism of speech isn't fully mature, which partly explains why it is something that children usually grow out of, but it can be frustrating and make a child withdrawn and lacking in confidence. Stressful situations can exacerbate the problem, but there is much encouragement a parent can give.

- **Listen attentively.** To maintain his confidence listen when your child is trying to say something without rushing, interrupting, or finishing his sentence.
- **Children's thoughts are often quicker than their speech**, so make sure neither you nor any older siblings finish your child's phrases.
- **Slow down your child** by taking the pressure off him: nod slowly and speak at the same pace.

Effective parenting

There is much that you can do through daily activities to stimulate his language development. The most important thing is to listen and respond appropriately to your child and to make sure that you spend time listening to and talking with him. Look at books together that may explore new ideas and emotional content (*see also box, right*). Get into the habit of naming objects, and talk as you dress him – for example, say you are putting on his red striped T-shirt and green socks. This all helps build his vocabulary.

Imaginative play

The development of language and imaginative play are interlinked for a young child. Pretending to be Mommy going to the store, for example, is one of the key ways in which young children learn to extend their language. The useful interaction between a child and his parent or caregiver, who can stimulate ideas on which the child can build, is also extremely beneficial. So learning to be imaginative is to the advantage of every child because it contributes to his or her creative intelligence.

Television and computers

Apart from occasionally allowing your child to watch an age-appropriate program, television isn't recommended since children find speech too difficult to follow, making it effectively a language-free form of entertainment. If your child spends a large proportion of his time watching television, it could have a negative effect on his language development, so monitor the time he spends watching it.

Even very young children can manage to use a word processor or computer. As with television, extended periods of unsupervised time can be detrimental, so spend just short periods of time with your child at the computer, letting him get a feel for it.

Reading

Books provide peaceful entertainment and encourage your child to focus on words; the ideas, emotional content and new words stimulate conversation. They may include new words that extend your child's vocabulary. Children's librarians can help you choose appropriate stories.

★ Listening to stories helps concentrate on the human voice and trains the brain to hear different letter sounds.

★ Rereading the same books entails the necessary repetition of words and the opportunity to ask questions about events in a book and what happens next, which helps develop language, and fosters a healthy emotional development in your child through the bonding process. Stories also introduce new ideas and emotional concepts.

★ Reading to your child fosters a healthy imagination, helps him build up relationships, and can create a warm, caring, and verbally confident child.

Safety

Safety is still a big issue for this age group, especially since your child is becoming more physically independent. This new independence usually isn't yet matched by an ability to think ahead or judge what is dangerous.

Your child's sense of spatial awareness, which enables her to judge distances or surrounding areas accurately, is still developing and she has only a limited memory of previous events from which to learn. In addition, she has a natural curiosity and inclination to explore that often overcomes what you may have told her not to do. This isn't deliberately disobedient behavior, it's just how small children find out about their world.

Take some practical steps to ensure that your child's environment is as safe as possible. Accidents sometimes happen, but you can avoid unnecessary mishaps with a little forethought and preparation. You will need to make sure that your home is as safe as you can make it. To avoid constantly having to tell your child not to touch certain things, make items such as electrical wall outlets safe, or move breakables out of reach, and get down to your child's level to see what other issues may arise.

It is important to instill a sense of self-responsibility about safety rules, too. These need to be reiterated again and again, but don't hover constantly over your child. Also decide which areas of safety are nonnegotiable, such as always wearing seat belts in the car.

Safety at home and out and about

★ Fit childproof catches to doors and drawers, and use safety glass or safety film on glass doors.

★ Allow your child to test things out with your guidance, since this is the only way that she will, in time, learn to make judgments about what she can and can't manage. Constantly berating her to "be careful" implies that you feel she can't manage alone, so praise any tasks that she completes safely.

★ Establish nonnegotiable family safety rules, such as wearing seat belts in the car and always holding a grown-up's hand to cross a road. Rules such as these will hopefully instill a sense of caution and road awareness in your child.

★ Ensure that breakables and hot liquid are always out of reach.

★ Never leave a small child alone in a room with a fireplace.

★ Watch for "lookalike" hazards: pills and medicines that may look like candy; or cleaning fluids that may seem similar to bottles of drink. Keep all household products and medication out of children's reach.

How toddlers learn

Over the next exciting twelve months of change, your child's outlook on life will open up as she gains a greater sense of independence and begins to explore the wider world. And, as her levels of understanding and communication improve, so too will her enjoyment of special relationships within the family and with other children.

How toddlers learn skills

The biggest change you will probably notice in your child's abilities as she enters her third year has to do with her understanding of her own world and her relationship to it, including the people around her.

Newfound abilities

During this year your child's experience of the world around her will increase partly through the tremendous development she will make in her language skills. It's also important to ensure that your child has a warm, nurturing, emotionally stable environment in which she can safely explore the world around her.

You may find that your child is becoming interested in everything going on around her. By letting your child join in as much as possible with some of your everyday activities, she will learn new skills as well as enjoy your company. For example, let your child help you to tidy up in the house or to lay the table since this will help her hand-eye coordination and give her a natural feeling of independence.

At this age, it can be hard for small children to know how to wind down if they are tired or accept that something has to finish. You may find your child resists or rebels against ending a game she is enjoying because you have to go out, for example. It takes improving memory skills to understand that finishing something enjoyable doesn't mean that it can't be done again another day. Explain this to your child and allow her time to digest the idea.

24–36 months: your child's milestones

In terms of overall physical growth, which slows down between the second and third birthday, the most noticeable change is your child's body proportions. As her limbs lengthen and her muscles strengthen from being used, her posture becomes more upright, with a flatter tummy.

Coordination and balance

Your child's expanding physical abilities in turn give her increased coordination and balance. Now she can walk quickly, for example, or carry a toy in her hand as she walks.

By the end of this year you can expect your child to be able to:
- walk upstairs using alternate feet
- bend down to retrieve a toy without falling over
- pedal a tricycle
- use a crayon to copy a circle on a piece of paper
- turn the pages of a book one at a time
- rotate her wrist and unscrew jar tops.

Intellectual skills

Until this point, your child's physical development, and what she learned from it, gave her the impression that what happens in her world is the result of something she has done.

This self-oriented view of the world means that a child this age often takes things literally. She finds it difficult to differentiate between fantasy and reality: if you say, for example, "If you eat any more, you'll burst!" it is just possible, from her point of view, that this could happen.

Imaginative play also becomes important as your child tries to make sense of and seek explanations for events by acting them out, and learns to distinguish fact from fantasy.

By the end of this year your child should be able to:
- follow a two-part instruction
- speak in sentences of four or five words
- be understood by nonfamily members
- play imaginative games
- match an object to a picture in a book
- enjoy choosing or sorting toys
- understand the concept of "two."

Emotional development

With the development of the idea of the self, and of possessions, comes difficulty in sharing – either sharing you, or her possessions. As your child becomes more social, she'll start to anticipate events and express pleasure at certain activities, or begin to recognize particular children and grown-ups. Her emotional range is still broad, ranging from sheer

IMPROVING SKILLS
Your child's improving skills of observation and concentration will enable him to complete simple jigsaw puzzles.

delight to frustrated rage. By the end of this year you can expect your child to:
- spend time happily away from you
- express affection to you and to other close family members
- show interest in other children.

Making sense of it all

The journey that you take with your child over this year happens in fits and starts, and the challenge for you is to help your child make sense of it all through opportunity and activity, with you as her guide.

24 to 26 months

Your two-year-old's growing independence and the pleasure he derives from his discoveries makes this an exciting time. You can still expect his emotions to reflect just how he is feeling – which can range from sunny smiles to tears in the space of 10 minutes. Help your child make the most of his eagerness to learn by encouraging him to improve his fine motor skills or build up his vocabulary through activities that you can do together.

Physical development

Your two-year-old's physical ability has progressed, almost literally, in leaps and bounds over the last 12 months and now he can walk, run, and climb. What he needs over this next period are lots of opportunities to use his body and explore his capabilities, building greater strength in his limbs and increasing his coordination.

Hops, skips, and jumps

Although your child may be unable to continually jump and hop at this stage, for example, it isn't long before he will incorporate an occasional hop, skip, or jump as he runs or walks. At first these movements have their own momentum, making them easier to accomplish than when standing still.

Social and emotional skills

Emotionally, your two-year-old will still appear quite selfish. This is our adult interpretation of his behavior, of course, but his inclination will be always to put his needs first unless you keep gently encouraging him to think of others.

Sharing by example

Encouraging your child to share is part of his learning to consider other people. It will also help increase his socialization process, which is learned primarily through imitation. If he is treated with respect and affection, he will learn to treat others in the same way. And if you are overly concerned with the feelings of others at the diminishment of his own, this won't encourage positive self-esteem in him anyway. Other people are just as important as he is, but not more so.

At this age you may also have the advantage of your child wanting to please you, so through your relationship with him he can learn to extend his consideration to others around him. Focusing on this aspect will help him develop the idea that if something is nice for him, then it would be nice for someone else too.

Expressing emotion

You can expect spontaneous and genuine shows of affection from your child by this stage, especially if similar attention has been lavished on him. It makes it much easier for him to accept and value other people's feelings if he feels accepted and valued, too.

Try to watch the language you use when managing your child's emotional behavior. He is not being bad or naughty if he doesn't want to wait his turn in playing with a toy or a simple game, he merely needs a gentle reminder or explanation of

Learning concepts

During this period you will be able to see your child's understanding evolve as you watch him play and as you talk and explain things to him. For example, if he sees you put his teddy bear inside a box and you then ask, "Where is the teddy bear?", he will soon comprehend what it means for something to be inside the box Keep demonstrating and then explaining things to him, and he will gradually begin to understand more about how the world around him works.

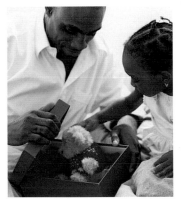

FINDING TEDDY
Demonstrating concepts in a practical and interesting way helps your child understand how things happen.

how the process works or what his part in playing with other children is. If he can't manage to grasp what you mean at first, wait with him, or try suggesting that he play beside you until he learns that taking turns is a positive thing to do.

Language and intellectual skills

Your child will make enormous progress throughout this year as his language skills develop and he begins to gather and express information in ways other than physical exploration alone. This aspect continues, too, of course, but it is the bringing together of his language and physical skills – for example, "When I do this, this happens" – that really helps his cognitive development.

Understanding concepts

The continued development of his memory, together with improving language skills, allows your child to begin to form mental images of how things happen, which leads to an understanding of concepts. Concepts are more the abstract ideas about how the world works – for example, the concepts of up and down, under and over, in and out.

You can help develop this skill by talking to your child about going inside your house, or show him how you put one stacking cup inside another or your purse inside your bag, for example (*see also box, p.41*).

Simple requests

Your child will now begin to understand your simple requests. He may find it difficult to understand a

Toy box

Picture lotto

Choose a chunky picture lotto game that your child can grasp easily, and with simple images. Use only a few pieces to begin with; as he gets older he can memorize more pictures.

Cassette player

Some children's cassette players enable a child to record their own voice talking and singing, or are even equipped with headphones for listening quietly to a favorite tape.

Tricycle

Tricycles are good for indoor and outdoor play. Let your child get used to pushing himself along with his legs and learn how to steer before showing him how to use the pedals.

Activities to develop skills

Giving your child lots of opportunities to explore what his body is capable of can help his physical development and his self-esteem. Help him develop his memory skills, too, with tapes and picture games.

★ Outdoor playgrounds with swings and slides are good because there are usually other children to share the experience, which also helps your child learn about taking turns.

★ Steady, durable tricycles with handlebars to steer but no pedals can provide your child with a different opportunity to exercise his legs, and develop the coordination needed to steer the handlebars. Help him with a gentle push to get started or use a

DANCING FOR JOY
Physical playtime, both indoors and outside, is great fun and essential for children since it helps them grow and develop.

complicated instruction, such as going into the hall, finding both of his shoes, and bringing them to you in the kitchen. But simple requests to do one thing at a time are easily within his grasp, such as asking him to bring you his shoes. This activity fosters a sense of general helpfulness and also helps him learn to act for himself, which builds his confidence in being able to manage small tasks, gives him a sense of self-esteem, and eventually leads to a degree of independence.

Making your own playdough

Making your own playdough saves time and money, and is fun. Your child may also enjoy helping you to mix and knead the dough once it is cool.

Cooked recipe:
7oz (200g) plain flour
3½oz (100g) salt
2tsp cream of tartar
1tbs vegetable oil
12oz (300ml) water

- Put the dry ingredients in a saucepan and gradually add the water, oil, and a little food coloring to color the dough. Cook over a low-medium heat, stirring continuously until stiff. Tip out, and then knead the dough once it has cooled down.
- Keep the dough in an airtight container in between play times. The salt will help preserve the mixture for a few weeks, and the salty taste will put off any children who may want to eat the dough.

---

tricycle with a long handle at the back to guide him along. Don't overdo the amount you help; provide enough momentum to get him started. Once he has mastered this he can try riding a tricycle using the pedals.

★ Matching shapes or pictures is an important observational skill that will help prepare your child for math. You may have previously given your child a shape-sorter box, then moved on to a tray puzzle, where he has to select and place a flat shape into its matching place on the board. Now this skill can be developed into a simple game of similarities and dissimilarities. This helps extend language skills to communicate ideas, observations, and feelings.

★ A cassette player designed to be used by little fingers will give your child access to music and favorite stories on tape. You may also like to record yourself reading a favorite story for your child and, if there are stories with which he is familiar, he can look at the book while listening to the tape. This will increase the access your child has to the spoken word. Learning to listen attentively will be of great benefit to him, especially when he joins a group of children at nursery school or playgroup. Make sure the volume can't be raised above a certain level, to avoid damaging his ears.

★ Soft, squidgy modeling clay is a delight in itself, and your child may enjoy just squeezing it through his fingers before getting involved in more imaginative play. Creating flat shapes and making impressions in the dough with pastry cutters – or even just making hand prints – allows him to explore all sorts of interesting possibilities with playdough.

ROLLING OUT DOUGH
Rolling playdough – either between the fingers or with a rolling pin – gives a child a huge amount of pleasure. Make sure you also provide a blunt plastic knife or cookie cutters to cut the dough.

26 to 28 months

Over the next months your child will begin to focus for longer periods on interactive activities that help expand her attention. During this time she will be capable of experiencing stronger emotions and will also be able to master skills through repetition. Although at first she may remain interested for only a comparatively short time, your gentle encouragement will help make her efforts all the more worthwhile.

Physical development

While your child's gross motor skills – such as walking and running – are improving, so, too, are her fine motor skills, enabling her to use her hands in specific ways to accomplish tasks.

Fine motor skills

At birth, your child's wrist and palm consisted of only three bones, in comparison to the 28 bones in an adult's hand. It isn't until the cartilage in a child's hand ossifies into bones that the brain's ability to influence the supporting muscles can mature. Once this happens, using tools (in your child's case, these are usually toys) becomes easier, whether it is a stick to beat a drum, a crayon for drawing, or a spoon for feeding herself.

As a baby, your child began by swiping at an object, then was able to grasp it with her whole fist, and now she can delicately pick up something quite small between her thumb and forefinger. Not only that, her ability to pick something up, twist her wrist, and place it carefully down again, is physically quite an achievement. Initially, all effort was put into trying to place and balance just one block on top of another, for example. Practice has made this easy, and now she may try to balance as many blocks as possible before they topple over – or are deliberately

knocked down! Thus her ability to pick up an object in her hand has matured immeasurably: she can now do this with greater accuracy and judge far more easily where to place the block so that it will balance.

Playing in the park also increases your child's motor skills, although she still needs close supervision since her energy levels and her expectations of her abilities can still get her into unexpected difficulties.

Social and emotional skills

The emotional range of a two-year-old is broad, extending from sheer delight to frustrated rage depending on your child's personality.

Managing emotion

While being able to express emotions freely is considered a healthy ability, what a child must learn is to manage her emotions and know which feelings are appropriate. This takes practice and she will need your help.

Children may feel overwhelmed by the force of their emotions sometimes, hence the full-blown tantrum. These situations need specific management skills (*see pp.18–19*), but it also helps to keep in mind what might trigger such extremes of emotion. Some children cannot manage emotionally as well as others when they are tired

or hungry, for example. It is worth remembering in the middle of an emotional maelstrom that your child is also capable of expressing positive emotions, such as happiness. So finding an activity to share that she

Repetition

You may find your child requests the same story book over and over again. Children of this age love repetition, and sometimes object if you deviate from exactly what is written. They may also remember or recognize the odd word, and notice it again if they then see the word printed somewhere else. You will probably find they like playing the same action songs, rhymes, and clapping games over again, too.

MEMORY GAMES
The visual stimulation and simple phrases of action games help develop a child's language and listening skills.

really enjoys and that allows her to express her happier side will help her self-esteem, and also increase your own pleasure.

Language and intellectual skills

Your child's understanding of the world continues to improve through her developing language and memory skills. Memory also helps in the development of her attention span as she begins to understand the concept of sequences of events.

Cause and effect

If you say you are going to read a story to your child, her memory of what this involves, and the pleasure she knows she will derive from it

when it happens, will make her more willing to focus on the book for the time it takes to read a story. She can then use this knowledge about what books involve, and how to enjoy them, to look at books by herself, developing her concentration and lengthening her attention span.

Over the last two years you may have collected numerous children's stories, from treasured first board books and favorite picture books to more sophisticated stories – all of which provide unique access to an imaginative world that helps your child learn about new ideas, cause and effect, feelings and facts, as well as developing concentration, learning how to listen, and extending the range of her vocabulary. This is the beginning of understanding about

learning to read, so it is important to encourage your child to develop a natural curiosity about books and stories, and to make the experience of reading a pleasurable one.

Improving concentration

You can also see the effectiveness of your child's memory at this age if you interrupt her activity to ask her a question about something else. She can focus on you and your question and then return to whatever it was she was doing. This is because she can now not only remember what she was doing, but what stage she had reached doing it.

Part of being able to develop this technique involves what psychologists call "selective or focal attention" – the ability to switch off from outside stimuli and concentrate on one thing at a time. One of the benefits of this is that concentration becomes easier if you can ignore other noise.

Some children can achieve a better level of concentration than others, so if your child finds it difficult to focus on something, reduce any background distractions or mask them by playing classical music at low volume. But remember that if you want your child to focus one-to-one on listening to your voice, either in conversation or by having a book read, make sure there is no background noise at all.

Toy box

Scrapbook materials
Choose round-ended scissors that are easy to open and shut with one hand, and a water-based glue that actually sticks but which can be washed off hands and clothes.

Painting equipment
Choose paint specially designed for young children and that will wash out of clothing. Thick finger paints in bright colors are the best choice. If you buy brushes, choose large brushes that are easy to grasp.

Books
Although your child will love reading the same stories over and over again, make sure you keep her stimulated by occasionally borrowing other books from your local library to vary the complexity of pictures and introduce new types of stories.

Activities to develop skills

Finger paints and gluing paper are a lovely way for children to make their mark. Be prepared for a mess and dress your child in old clothes, or use overalls. You can also help improve your child's coordination and imagination by encouraging her to continue playing with blocks, and try to spend time reading stories and looking at pictures together.

SHARED ACTIVITY
To begin with, your child may need a little help and encouragement to try finger painting.

MESSY HANDS
Praise your child's efforts, even if her first attempts are splotchy, and she'll soon gain the confidence to experiment.

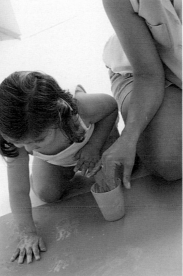

GLUING PAPER
Gluing paper is a skill in itself: your child needs to learn to adjust the amount of glue required to stick something down.

★ First attempts at hand painting don't need pristine paper — use the back of any junk mail or recycled computer printouts – but you do need to allow plenty of scope for experimentation. Help your child enjoy the process for its own sake, with colors and shapes; then, when the masterpiece is dry, stick it on the wall for everyone to enjoy. You can also chop a potato in half, cut a simple shape (like a circle or cross),

into the surface, and let your child dip it in paint to make potato prints. Or try using a sponge dipped into paint.

★ Colored blocks in different shapes and sizes will encourage your child's imagination. She may deliberately choose blocks of all one color, subconsciously sorting them to bring a sense of order. Rather than just put one block on top of another, she may start to build different shapes and create her own games.

★ Find time every day to sit and read books with your child. If you have children of different ages, it is possible to share a range of books, reading to your two-year-old while feeding your baby, for example, or choosing a book with enough of a story for an older child to enjoy as well. Carry a couple of favorites with you in your bag in case you have an unexpected wait somewhere.

★ Encourage your child's hand skills and hand–eye coordination by helping her make a scrapbook or a book of discarded or duplicate photos. Get her used to scissors by letting her cut colored paper into broad strips and squares, and include stickers and water-based glue. First attempts are often a messy business, but that's all part of the fun.

28 to 30 months

The human body is designed for motor activity, and young children in particular need to develop important physical skills such as coordination and balance, as well as improve their stamina and strength. In addition, the chance to master their physical abilities and skills helps enhance young children's self-esteem, muscle development, and coordination. It is important for children to have the opportunity to participate in physical activities under adult supervision, and to be encouraged to do so.

Physical development

Your child needs plenty of physical activity to help expend some of the enormous amounts of energy he exhibits at this age. The amount of exercise he gets helps his spatial understanding and, by extension, his balance and coordination skills.

Ball games

Playing outside with a ball can give enormous pleasure to an energetic two-and-a-half-year-old. Kicking the ball requires balance and coordination, while throwing it is really an extension of letting go, with a little force behind it. Catching, too, is a skill that has to be learned. Your child's first attempts will be inaccurate and haphazard, but with practice and praise he'll improve in time.

ACQUIRING THE SKILLS
Developing ball skills helps improve hand–eye coordination and increases the pleasure of new achievements that encourage physical self confidence.

Body and brain

Getting plenty of exercise not only burns off excess energy, it establishes a positive body image and a sense of self-esteem in your child's mind.

In addition, the connections built between neurones in the brain, known as neural pathways, are formulated by persistent physical, as well as cognitive, activity. This is why, once learned, we never forget how to ride a bicycle unless something interferes with those specific neural patterns imprinted in our brains. Therefore, a child needs practice in the larger physical skills – running, kicking, climbing, or pedaling a tricycle – to become competent, as well as build strength and use energy.

Exercising together

With concerns growing about today's rising rates of childhood obesity, our sedentary lifestyles, and children's lack of exercise, it is as well to foster an enjoyment of exercise. Let your child walk rather than take the car, allowing him to sit in his stroller if he gets tired, or park farther away from the stores than usual and walk there.

Social and emotional skills

You may find that as your child becomes more social he starts to anticipate events and express

pleasure at one activity over another. He may also begin to express his excitement when he sees a friend he recognizes or enjoys playing with.

Other relationships

Forming attachments outside the immediate family circle is evidence of your child's widening emotional development. He is starting to make relationships based on his own positive feelings about being a person, independent of you.

It is important to try to validate your child's emotions, even if doing so sometimes seems at odds with your feelings. With his improving language skills, articulating how he feels about someone, or something, becomes a greater possibility. He may not know what he feels at first, but you can help him explore his emotions. Don't disregard him, tell him not to be silly, or ignore the situation if he appears hesitant about playing with another child, for example. Gently determine what it is that he doesn't feel comfortable about.

Expressing pleasure

In the same way, when a person or an event generates particular pleasure, ask your child what it is that feels good about the experience. Use this opportunity to talk to him about feelings but keep it simple. By being attuned to your child's feelings and acknowledging them, and encouraging him to articulate them when he's ready, you are paving the way to him being able to learn how to explore and express his own feelings.

Other people's feelings

If your child can learn at this early age that his feelings are valued, it will eventually enable him to consider other people's feelings in the same way. Respecting your child's feelings in turn teaches him that respecting another individual's emotions is equally important.

Language and intellectual skills

Since memory is such an important part of what helps children develop intellectually, it is worth helping your child improve his memory skills.

Show and tell

At this stage it is still easier for children to remember language that is reinforced by physical activity, such as action songs (*see also box, p.45*). In the same way, when you tell your child how to do something, show

him at the same time – turn the page of a book carefully, or close a door gently, for example. This is especially important when your child grapples with abstract concepts.

Creating an impact

For all of us, remembering routines that happen every day is harder than remembering one-time events. You may notice that if you ask your child what he had for breakfast – even if it was only an hour ago – he may look at you blankly since the food he eats every day is not of

Activities to develop skills

Encourage young children at this age to engage in pretend play, since it is an absorbing way for them to develop their imaginations – likewise with toy cars and train sets, and plastic blocks and models.

★ Playing out the simple routines in their lives helps children make sense of events and prepares them for more complicated pretend play,

which in turn stimulates their imagination. Pretend games are also the way in which young children begin to develop an understanding of what is

TEA FOR THREE
When pretend games happen, they are often the end result of remembering something that has happened before and exploring what might yet happen.

real and what is not – the difference between fact and fantasy. Playing with a tea set, for example, involves all sorts of remembered events of preparing and drinking tea – it may even be too hot to drink! Children recognize that drinking tea or coffee is a social event, usually drunk sitting down, sometimes with a friend. A child will act all of this out in his game, usually talking it through as he does so. He'll probably be equally happy playing on his own with some toys, or with you or perhaps a friend.

★ Toy cars or a simple train set can give both boys and girls great pleasure, so always encourage imaginative play. What may differentiate girls and boys in the way they play with these toys is how they develop this into their own particular imaginative game: pushing

much consequence to him. But if you ask him what he had for lunch on his last visit to his grandma's house, he may easily remember when he returns there and point to a cabinet, for example. Children are very much "of the moment," and remembering the mundane holds comparatively little interest for them. Something that may have been planned, discussed, and involved a change in the normal routine becomes an exciting event, and thus has a greater impact on a child.

Toy box

Balls
Buy a medium-sized, lightweight ball that your child can easily wrap his arms around to hold securely. Soft tennis balls are another option.

Tea set
A brightly colored, well-made plastic tea set will give hours of pleasure. Make sure the pieces are sturdy

enough for little hands, and not so flimsy that they keep toppling over.

Plastic bricks
The chunkier the plastic pieces are, the more chance your two-year-old will have of being able to use his coordination skills and the strength in his hands to fit blocks together without becoming frustrated.

---

the cars around, imagining different scenarios, and acting them out. You can buy special mats with a road layout marked on them for an added focus for play, but these aren't essential items.

★ Larger plastic bricks are easier for little fingers to use. A good selection of bricks is an ideal toy for both boys and girls of this age, and can be played with in a variety of different ways: building toys, houses, and scenes, and incorporating play figures and animals encourages all sorts of imaginative play. Children's creativity is stimulated when they are allowed to use their imagination. Take your lead from your child to assess the degree of help needed and always encourage creative play; resist any urge to teach him or control his playtime in any way.

BUMPER TO BUMPER
A good selection of toy cars provides opportunities for shared play as your two-year-old begins to play with, rather than beside, another child.

CAPTURING THE IMAGINATION
Although by no means an exclusively male pastime, playing with toy cars may hold boys' interest for longer and from an earlier age.

30 to 32 months

During these early years you are your child's first teacher and her most sensitive guide, and time spent together is invaluable. Even when life is very busy, finding a moment to spend time alone together to give your child your undivided attention will give you both pleasure. Reading is one important way that you can provide physical reassurance and comfort, the familiarity of a favorite story, and the one-to-one attention your child needs to flourish.

Physical development

Given the opportunity, it's amazing what a difference practice can make to your child's ability to use her hands proficiently.

Hand skills

It may be interesting to note that most Chinese children at this age are competent at using chopsticks, since they have had to learn to do so in order to feed themselves – something those of us who find chopsticks hard to use may think extraordinary!

What you can expect of your child now, though, is that she uses her hands to do a variety of different things, from carefully turning the page of a book to holding a pencil or unscrewing a jar. Practice undoing snaps on clothes, for instance, can help her fine motor skills and develop her independence. Help her by selecting the sort of clothes that enable her to manage dressing as much as possible by herself. This will also help her competence and her self-esteem.

Growing in confidence

Another measure of your child's increased physical skills is her ability to balance blocks one on top of the other. When your child was in her second year, learning to balance just one block at a time on top of

another seemed quite a feat. But now that she is in her third year, she should be able to manage to stack at least six blocks.

This maturing of fine motor skills helps in all sorts of ways, including encouraging your child to develop the self-confidence to try other things that were once quite difficult. Seeing her own progress, and enjoying the pleasure and satisfaction that it brings, encourages her to try other new activities.

Social and emotional skills

Your child has probably developed quite a clear idea of what possessions are, but she still needs reminding that she can share what she has.

A child's viewpoint

Understanding what's "mine" at this age can result in a certain amount of possessiveness in children. However, all this is really just part of how they view the world around them from their own, very singular, point of view. What is needed is for you to act as a guide to your child: by helping her open up her focus and incorporate a wider viewpoint.

Learning respect

Most of this social behavior is learned by example, so if you want your child to share you will also have to watch your own possessiveness! Saying "Don't touch that, it's precious," may be a way of avoiding something getting broken, but it also conveys the idea that if

Awareness of self

Your child probably now knows that she is a girl – or he is a boy – and can distinguish between the sexes, although she may not always know why. She will also be able to refer to herself as "I" and may be able to describe herself in simple sentences: "I am hungry," for example. This growing awareness of self began months before, but its expression is now becoming clearer, and as your child's language skills become better she may be able to convey her thoughts more easily.

ROLE MODEL
While traditional stereotypes are no longer the norm, children often tend to look to role models of the same sex.

it's yours, your child can't have it. So, by extension, if that toy is your child's, why should she let another child have a turn with it? It helps if you can take the time to explain why it is important to respect other people's possessions so that she will respect yours while still being able to share.

Language and intellectual skills

By now your child's vocabulary may include as many as 200–300 words. She may also be using connecting words between phrases such as "and," while also adding details through description. Bilingual children may initially have a smaller vocabulary base, and at first tend to mix words from each language when they speak, but they will soon catch up with their peers.

Asking questions

With this acquired vocabulary comes the question, "Why?" This process of questioning is valuable to your child since it helps her understand and is likely to continue for many months. Answer simply, allowing for development of thought and further questions from your child, rather than overwhelm her with a complicated explanation. Answering a two-year-old's incessant questioning is an art, and there can't be many parents who haven't resorted occasionally to saying, "Because I say so!" However, be prepared for the comeback, "Why?" You may even want to respond with your own question in a friendly tone: "What do you think?" Your child now also understands quite complex instructions from you, although she may choose not to respond!

Developing conversations

Attending a play group or a nursery school is an important opportunity for children to enjoy interacting with each other and develop their own communication.

Your child may also keep up a running monologue to herself to help her organize her thoughts, or have pretend conversations with a teddy bear or doll. It can bring you up short when you hear your child say sternly, "No!" to her toys!

Speaking clearly

Children of this age may still speak unclearly or mispronounce words. This may be connected to the development of facial muscles, and can be helped by making sure that you give your child lots of foods that require chewing. This helps exercise the same muscles needed for speech. If your child still mispronounces most words, it is important to check first with your pediatrician that she hasn't suffered any hearing loss. Also check that any background noise is turned off when you spend one-to-one time together.

Toy box

Dolls

You can now buy dolls with appropriate clothes that are specially made to help young children learn about the process of dressing and undressing. Playing with dolls will stimulate a child's imagination and also encourage role-playing games.

Picture dominos

Make sure that the dominos are large enough for young children to pick up and put down easily.

Jigsaw puzzles

Choose puzzles with a maximum of six or seven pieces so that the task of fitting everything together is not too daunting for your child. Well-made wooden jigsaw puzzles with clear, simple pictures are most appropriate for small fingers and hopefully will hold a child's attention.

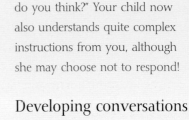

Activities to develop skills

Simple jigsaw puzzles are an excellent way of training your child's eye to recognize matching shapes and to look at how things fit together. You can also help her manage a small task and improve her fine motor skills by giving her a doll to undress. Try playing singing games to improve her ability to listen to different sounds and follow rhythms.

★ Introduce the idea of rhythm to your child by beating time. Pick out the rhythm of different words, or combinations of words, for example, the rhythm in your child's name: Martin becomes Mar-tin, Samantha becomes Sam-an-tha, and so you introduce the idea of syllables with a game. Maybe an older sibling could play an instrument while you and your two-year-old beat time clapping your hands or tapping glasses filled with different measures of water.

★ Getting dressed and undressed is a routine part of your child's activity, and something she may be happy to attempt on her own. It can provide the chance to learn to undo various clothes fastenings – snaps and zippers, which require small, precise movements of the fingers. But these are skills of great value, and something your child needs to be competent at doing in due course. It also allows her to develop the sort of confidence needed to be able to manage small tasks alone, which will stand her in good stead when she has to manage away from one-to-one support – perhaps when she starts nursery school.

★ You may also like to try playing picture dominos and matching games with your child. Matching pictures demands observation and memory skills and improves her ability to spot similarities. While she is still too young to play this game on her own, she may enjoy playing alongside you.

BRAIN TEASER
Children love the challenge of completing jigsaw puzzles and can become quickly absorbed in their task.

★ Simple jigsaw puzzles take the process of matching up shapes to another stage, since they require good observation skills. Children find great satisfaction in trying to find the right piece and put it in the right place. Learning to look at something in this very specific way is also good training for the identification of letter shapes later on. Jigsaw puzzles also require focus, concentration, and a logical thought process, but it doesn't feel like that to a child — it's just a game!

MAKING MUSIC
Encourage an older sibling to play a simple tune so that your two-year-old can copy the rhythm by tapping glasses.

32 to 34 months

Quiet times are important for small children to have as part of their normal routine. It allows them the opportunity to be imaginative, creative, and develop new ideas of their own. Don't be tempted to fill every waking moment of your child's day with a planned activity or an organized event. It's important for him to be allowed to be creative and to learn how to develop his own imagination.

Physical development

Your two-year-old can now build on the strength he has developed so far in his limbs to climb up and down stairs, walk on tiptoe, and control his hand movements more accurately.

Balance and flexibility

If you live in a house with a flight of stairs, your two-year-old may now be getting used to going safely up and down them, although you should never leave him to climb or descend the steps on his own.

If you do not have stairs in your home, your child will inevitably have had less practice at this skill. However, he is probably now beginning to climb stairs stepping up one foot at a time rather than taking just one step at a time.

Improving motor skills

Jumping with two feet may now be possible for your child, although he may still be rather flat-footed. You might like to suggest games that encourage him to walk on tiptoe in bare feet. This activity strengthens his feet and gives flexibility and balance. Your child may also be getting more competent at washing and drying his hands. Some fine motor skills, such as eating with a spoon or fork, are also improving, but may still be a little haphazard.

Social and emotional skills

Attention-seeking behavior in two-year-old children can take different forms, and having a tantrum is often one of them.

Displaying emotions

At this age, aggressive behavior can be new and threatening and can be due to changes or events, or a learned response. If they surface in a previously peaceable child, consider why his behavior may have changed. Seek appropriate help from your healthcare professional if you feel that his behavior is not appropriate..

Emotional frustration

It's important to work out why a child responds to situations in this antisocial way. This can be difficult if having a tantrum gets him what he wants in the short term. Tantrums are usually linked to a child's frustration and an inability to communicate effectively. A two-year-old cannot do all the things he wants, or fully understand that there are things he cannot have. Check if he is overtired or hungry, or feels threatened in some way or needs positive attention.

Positive attention

Children have an emotional need for a lot of attention and, while positive attention is better than negative, they tend not to make that distinction – any attention will do if a child feels he isn't getting enough.

The challenge of parenting is being attuned to your child so that you can try to accommodate his needs as they change. The basic principle is to

Hand–eye coordination

At first, threading spools or large buttons demands good hand–eye coordination and a considerable amount of concentration. However, this is a rewarding activity since it affords the chance not just to thread objects together, but to choose the sequence of colors and shapes.

THREADING SPOOLS
If you don't have time to make your own shapes by cutting circles and squares in colored card with a hole at the center, you can buy colored spools and thread.

try to ignore negative behavior and to be generous in your reward of good behavior. So, when you have to deal with any aggressive behavior in your child, make sure that you pay attention to, and reward any occasions of, positive behavior with praise.

Also give your child specific feedback on his behavior so that he learns what is and what isn't considered desirable. You might say, for example, "Thank you for sharing your books," or "I like it when you play gently with your sister".

Language and intellectual skills

Your child may now be beginning to grasp the concept of simple number sequences and different categories.

Number sequences

Your child's knowledge of numbers began when you first sang number rhymes to him, although it wouldn't have been clear then what these words represented. Through your frequent repetition, your child may have learned to "count" to five, or 10,

although in reality he has just been repeating a sequence of sounds.

Now he will begin to use these familiar words to represent the more tangible concept of counting. The development of this understanding begins with forming groups, or sequences, of objects. Just counting three cars or two spoons is a start. Your child may also grasp the idea of different categories soon: 10 plastic animals in total, but three cows, five pigs, and two horses. You may even find him repeating numbers and number sequences in his games.

Activities for developing skills

Imaginative play is very important for young children. Through it they learn to work out certain abstract concepts, act out story lines, "try on" different ideas, explore feelings and ways of behaving – all within their own imaginations.

★ Playing with other children is a learned skill, and is all about socializing, taking turns, and thinking about others. Help your child learn these skills by playing simple board games that are appropriate to his age group and encourage him to take turns. In addition, playing a counting game enables you to help him learn about numbers plus their names and sequences. If you play board games, focus on the pleasure and excitement of playing the game, irrespective of who wins, so that winning is not your child's only achievement when playing. It is more important at this

age to have fun than to focus on the desire to win.

★ Reading books are probably a regular feature in your child's life now, not just at bedtimes but also at other times of the day. Remember that small children enjoy clear, attractive pictures and, by this stage, will probably listen to quite a sophisticated story line. Looking at books alone is still something to be encouraged. If you are unsure which books might be appropriate for your child, ask a children's librarian to recommend different titles, authors, and illustrators. Some children's libraries may also have some special

SOCIAL GATHERING
Children may need a little encouragement to begin playing with each other, but they soon become involved in imaginary games.

storytelling sessions and other entertaining book-related activities that your child can enjoy.

★ All young children should be encouraged to play games that rely

Nursery rhymes

Have you ever wondered why parents pass down favorite nursery rhymes through the generations? Perhaps it's from an intuitive knowledge that talking to your child helps him develop speech, but the repetition of nursery rhymes is also a very useful preparation for reading. The constant repetition of the rhymes in early life means that your child becomes familiar with different word sounds. They also engage his attention, helping him pick up information about language and how it works.

Toy box

Simple board games

Focus on simple games with your child, such as buying a durable board game that is clearly marked as being appropriate for his age group. Go slowly and patiently as you play with him, and you may find that he soon begins to pick up the rules of the game.

Dress-up box

It is worth keeping a large box full of a selection of old grown-ups' castoffs and dress-up clothes for children to play with. Encourage them to think imaginatively about how they can adapt the clothes to suit who they want to pretend to be.

on their own internal resources, and dressing-up games help to stimulate this ability. Dressing up also makes a game of developing the necessary skills your child needs to learn in order to be able to dress herself.

A big square of material can instantly become a princess's cloak, a magician's cape, a magic carpet, a baby's blanket, or Red Riding Hood's granny's shawl. Adults' clothes and accessories such as old hats or high-heeled shoes are another great attraction. Shop-bought outfits, perhaps based on popular fictional characters, are also an option, as are doctors' and nurses' outfits and other costumes. As your child grows, he may find more and more enjoyment in his repeated imaginative games, especially when other children are prepared to join in and play with him.

ROLE-PLAYING
Most children love dressing up, and enjoy wearing the odd grown-up castoff as they act out their pretend role-play games.

34 to 36 months

Your almost-three-year-old is becoming much more obviously her own person now, with her own developing interests and opinions. Her personality is also becoming more clearly established, and, while she may share certain characteristics with other family members, she is learning to experiment and express her own ideas. However, your child still needs all your encouragement, affection, and security, so don't entrust her with older siblings without you being there to supervise, for example.

Physical skills

As they near their third birthday, most children are now physically proficient in the large motor skills of running, walking, and climbing. If you feel that your child isn't perhaps as physically competent as her peers, it may be that she needs more practice to develop these skills.

Individual development

Some children may seem physically less able than others because often they are impatient to get from one place to another, or achieve a specific task; they may manage better if they slow down and take things more gently. Other children can be very impulsive and don't allow themselves time to assess physical risk, so, again, they may need some encouragement to slow down a little. If they show little natural fear or reservation, they may need help in understanding that what they are doing could put themselves at risk.

Structured activities

For a parent, it may feel like a natural inclination to reduce the level of physical activity in a child who appears less physically able, but guard against this tendency as it won't help the child. In fact, increasing the amount of structured activities to help your child learn to

manage physical skills more easily will be to her advantage. As long as it could help her in an uncompetitive and fun way, think about whether she may benefit from joining a gymnastics or dance class for young children at your local

The concept of time

Your child may be advanced enough in her understanding now to grasp the abstract concept of time – before and after, for instance. She may now understand you if you say she can get down and play "after you've finished your lunch." This understanding is possible because of her developing experience and her memory of what happens during the course of her day.

MEALTIME
Repeated activities such as mealtimes and bedtime help define the course of the day for young children

sports center. Remember to keep giving her lots of encouragement to raise her self-esteem.

Social and emotional skills

Your child should now be reasonably happy to be separated from you with a familiar caregiver for an extended period of time, though some children may manage this progression with less anxiety than others.

Separation

In order to be able to separate happily from you, your child needs to be able to hold onto the thought of you and know that you will return to her, something which is learned partly through experience. How you handle the separation will also convey to your child what is expected of her. If you appear confident that she will manage and be safe without you, you will convey to her your confidence in her ability to manage. If you are anxious or diffident, she may well pick up on this emotion, which might make it more difficult for her to feel confident without you.

Practical measures

Whether your child is about to start nursery school or is getting used to being with a baby-sitter, there are

Activities to develop skills

Your child's first scribbles with wax crayons have now become more deliberate, controlled, and influenced by what she is trying to achieve. She still enjoys learning through play, so continue to keep her stimulated.

★ Picture lotto is a wonderful game for all kinds of reasons. It can be played by two or more people so it encourages the process of sharing, taking turns, and developing conversation. It also helps develop a child's visual memory skills.

★ Bath time is a good wind-down at the end of the day, but it can also include pleasurable activities such as pouring water from one container to another, playing with bath toys, singing songs and rhymes, and chatting with you about the events

of your child's day. Foam letters can also provide an easy way to introduce first letter shapes that can be touched and moved around. Handling something actually helps a young child memorize it better, so these large letters and numbers can help your child identify and remember them. Choose letters that are lower case, not capitals. Introducing the letters to your child just by naming them is enough at this stage. Then let her add them to her collection of toys in the bath to have fun with them.

★ By the end of your child's third year, outdoor play will not only be a source of pleasure for her but a way in which she can run off some of her abundant energy. It is much easier

PICTURE LOTTO
This game helps improve a child's observational skills as he matches pictures and develops an eye for slight differences in shape, color, or form.

to tolerate inactivity and focus on something if there has been a chance to expend some energy first. A daily excursion to a park, almost whatever the weather, is a change of scene and an opportunity to exercise those growing limbs. Regular exercise also encourages a child's appetite, and helps her sleep well.

★ Your child will probably now love to make pictures with paints, crayons, or even washable felt-tip pens. While she may still sometimes use either hand, it is likely that she will now use just one hand rather than the other. Movements are still big, but she may be able to copy some basic shapes – a circle, square, or even a triangle, for example. Help her develop a good pencil grip by giving her triangular-shaped crayons, since they will encourage a tripod grasp.

PAINTING SKILLS
In addition to improving his control and flexibility, painting helps a child learn to express himself through shape and color.

some practical measures you should keep in mind to make things bearable: ensure that your child understands exactly who is going to care for her and that she realizes they are a familiar face; be confident yourself that you trust and feel relaxed with whoever is left in charge; reassure your child that you are coming back; and then leave her on a positive note.

Other practical measures to help your child feel secure include giving her a photograph of you or perhaps allowing her to take a security object along with her for a while.

Maintaining trust

Don't be tempted to try to avoid a scene by slipping away from her without saying goodbye, since this will betray her trust in you. Even if she appears unable to manage without you, remember that she will be fine and will soon learn that she can manage her feelings without you being present, which in turn will build her confidence.

Feeling secure

While most children will separate quite happily once they feel secure – and are also happy to see their parents again – if you find that your child has been upset while you've been away, don't leave her for more than 20 minutes at a time until she really feels settled in her environment.

Language and intellectual skills

Your child should now be able to converse with you in short sentences rather than just in phrases, and she may now be able to continue talking about a topic for a short period.

Personal references

Your child will probably now refer to herself as "I" rather than by her name, say "you" rather than use the third person, and refer to friends and family by name. This demonstrates how her cognitive skills have advanced over the year in identifying herself as an individual within her family, and referring to herself as such. By the age of three most children's speech should be at least 60 percent

understandable to strangers. If, however, your child is becoming more difficult to understand or is saying less, arrange to have her hearing checked by a healthcare professional.

Visual memories

As her language skills improve, you will notice how good your child's memory and observation skills are becoming. Children have very visual memories, so if your child has a broad range of vocabulary you may be surprised by how much detail she can give you about something she has seen or heard. Encourage your child to develop this skill by asking her to describe events or experiences in more detail and ask simple questions about what she saw or how she felt.

Toy box

Picture lotto

If you have already begun playing a simple version of picture lotto with your child, you may want to buy a slightly more sophisticated version of the game if she is becoming proficient at it. Or make your own version of picture lotto using pictures cut from magazines and glued onto square pieces of card.

Foam letters

Many toy shops now sell containers of foam letters and numbers that will stick to the side of the bath tub when wet. Choose large rather than small pieces.

Pens and paper

Buy chunky pens or triangular-shaped crayons and bright paper to give your child many hours of fun

Index

Acknowledgments

Credits
Jacket photo: Britt J. Erlanson-Messens/Image Bank; **jacket design:** Nicola Powling
Indexer: Hilary Bird; **proof-reader:** Nikky Twyman
Models: Simon with Lauren Murrell, Deborah with Aaron Bright, Mr and Mrs Perez, George with Sophia Sirius, Tony with Christina and Louise Aquino, Sima and Tim with Danielle and Tal Randall, Gaynor with Oliver Benveniste, Sue with Anya Dziewulski, Deborah with Sadie Seitler, Meena with Shaun MacNamara, Jane with Luke Rimell, Cheryl and John with Yasmin Weekes, Orlean with Ethan Stennett, Sibel with Lara Peck, Teresa with Isabelle; **hair and make–up:** Tracy Townsend

Consultants
Warren Hyer MRCP is Consultant Pediatrician at Northwick Park and St. Mark's Hospitals, Harrow, and Honorary Clinical Senior Lecturer, Imperial College of Science, Technology and Medicine.

Penny Tassoni is an education consultant, author and trainer. Penny lectures on a range of childhood studies courses and has written five books, including *Planning, Play and the Early Years*.

Picture Credits
Picture researcher: Cheryl Dubyk-Yates
Picture librarian: Hayley Smith

The publisher would like to thank the following for their kind permission to reproduce their photographs:
(abbreviation key: t=top, b=bottom, r=right, l=left, c=centre)

Retna Pictures Ltd: Ewing Reeson 49bl. **Gettyone stone:** 9tr.
Jacket photo: Jason Homa/Image Bank

All other images © Dorling Kindersley. For further information see: www.dkimages.com